ENDORSEMENTS

If I had to describe It's Gonna Be Alright in one word, it would be profound. I was surprised at how effortlessly Tiffany's words pulled me in. From the moment I opened the book, it was difficult to put down . . . because the story spoke to my spirit.

Through every chapter, Tiffany's honesty, raw emotion, and transparency were not only powerful, they were necessary for healing. She doesn't just recount events, she reflects, empowers, and reminds readers of their own strength. She closes each chapter with hope and wisdom, urging women to believe in their worth and future.

Chapter 18, in particular, felt like the spiritual anchor of the book. I truly believe that nothing and no one goes in vain. Everything Tiffany went through was part of her process to learn, grow, and rediscover herself. Her strength, faith, and willingness to share the most vulnerable parts of her life make this book a gift.

Tiffany, you are a warrior. You've done something incredibly brave, writing a book and bearing your soul for others to learn and heal from. It's Gonna Be Alright is a book that will resonate deeply with women who are still trying to find their voice, their strength, and their peace.

NERRISSA J.

Isaiah 61:3: "To console those who mourn in Zion, to give them beauty for ashes, the oil of joy for mourning, the garment of praise for the spirit of heaviness."

I wept hard reading this beautiful body of work, not just because of my love for you, but also because I can heavily relate. And here you came again throwing me a life jacket.

I see you more clearly than I ever have. I see that woman who guided me through every area of my life while navigating hers in the dark, and I still say, "I wanna be like her when I grow up." The resilience after pain, the strength, the grit, the fight for your place in this earth, be it quiet or loud.

I still believe God sent you to me, and even in this moment used you to share your story with me and help me be free. I finished it today, and today God allowed me to heal. Thank you always. I love you for free.

T. BURKE

From the introduction through the final chapter, the author gifts us with the ugly parts of life and marriage women are often too ashamed to share. "Healing doesn't come from wanting someone else to change, it comes from recognizing you deserve more," says Civers.

Thank you for telling your truth and giving readers the blueprint for choosing joy.

LASHAWN BUTLER-FRANCIS, LCSW AUTHOR & THERAPIST

IT'S GONNA BE ALRIGHT

A MEMOIR OF HEALING FROM EMOTIONAL ABUSE, DIVORCE, AND DIVINE TRANSFORMATION

TIFFANY M. CIVERS

EDITED BY
NICOLE QUEEN

VISION PUBLISHING
HOUSE

Vision Publishing House
support@vision-publishinghouse.com
www.vision-publishinghouse.com

ISBN: 978-1-955297-95-0 (print)
LCCN: 2025916251

DISCLAIMER

This book is a personal memoir based on my own experiences, reflections, and perceptions. The events, emotions, and situations described are written from my perspective and represent my truth as I experienced it. While every effort has been made to preserve the authenticity of these experiences, some names, identifying details, locations, and characteristics have been changed to protect privacy.

This book is not intended to defame, harm, or malign any individual or group. It is meant to serve as a source of healing, empowerment, and awareness for those who have experienced similar situations. The views and opinions expressed are solely my own and do not reflect the views of any specific organization, institution, or entity.

This book should not be considered professional legal, psychological, or therapeutic advice. Readers experiencing distress are encouraged to seek support from licensed professionals.

This book is a memoir. It reflects the author's present recollections of experiences over time. Some names, dates, locations, and characteristics have been changed, some time frames have been compressed, and some dialogue has been re-created.

This book represents the personal views and opinions of the author and does not reflect the positions or opinions of any organization, institution, or individual with which the author is affiliated. The content presented herein is based on the author's perspective and interpretation of the subject matter. Neither the publisher, distributor, nor any associated parties shall be held responsible for any consequences arising from the opinions or interpretations expressed within this book.

To my daughter…

From the moment you came into this world, you have been one of my greatest blessings. I have watched you grow into a strong, compassionate, and resilient woman, and I am endlessly proud of you. You are the reflection of everything I prayed for. You are proof that strength runs through our bloodline. You are a reminder that love, when given freely and unconditionally, has the power to heal.

This journey has been long, and at times, painful. But if there is one thing I want you to take from this, it is this: you are enough. You do not have to sacrifice yourself for love. You do not have to shrink to be accepted. You do not have to prove your worth to anyone.

I wrote this book so that if you ever find yourself questioning your power, you can open these pages and remember you come from a long line of warriors. No matter what life throws your way, it's gonna be alright.

I love you endlessly.

And one day, she discovered that the
pieces of her pain were never meant to break her.
They were meant to build her.
With God, she didn't just survive, she rose.

CONTENTS

Foreword   xiii
Cassandra Pryor

Preface   xv
Who is Tiffany M. Civers?   xvii
Introduction   xxi

PART ONE
THE BREAKING

1. The Foundation   3
2. The Day I Learned to Disappear   7
3. Healing My Inner Child   13
4. The Awakening   17
5. The Pain Was Always There   21
   Raw Emotions   27
6. The Beginning of the War   29
7. The Twist from Reality   37
8. Postpartum Neglect   41
   Raw Emotions   47

PART TWO
THE AWAKENING

9. Reclaiming Myself   53
10. The Breakthrough: Choosing Me   59
11. God's Promise and the Price of Freedom   65
    Raw Emotions   69
12. The Silence That Spoke the Loudest   71
13. Remembering Joy   77
14. Concealing the Humiliation   81
15. Giving Yourself the Same Empathy You Gave Others   87
    Raw Emotions   91

PART THREE
THE BECOMING

16. The Power of No Contact, Reclaiming My Peace   95
17. Embracing the Unknown   99
    Raw Emotions   103

18. Building Healthy Relationships with Boundaries 107
19. To the Woman Who Feels Stuck 111
20. Tears of Joy and the Power of Surrender 115
21. Embracing Triumph, Transformation, & Faith 119
Raw Emotions 123

Stepping into the Light 125
Resources 127

Acknowledgments 129
About the Author 133

FOREWORD

CASSANDRA PRYOR

In a world where challenges often feel insurmountable, there are those rare souls who not only navigate their storms, but also light the way for others.

Tiffany is one such remarkable woman—a beacon of hope whose selflessness and resilience inspire everyone around her. As I reflect on the journey encapsulated in her heartfelt book, *It's Gonna Be Alright*, I am both humbled and honored to pen these words.

Tiffany's story is one of triumph over adversity, of emerging from the shadows and surviving the tumult of divorce. It is a narrative that many women can resonate with, as it bravely exposes the deep wounds and struggles that all too often remain hidden. But Tiffany does not merely recount her pain; she transforms it into a powerful testimony of healing and faith. Through her own trials, she embodies the essence of perseverance and strength, proving that even in our darkest moments, there is light to be found.

What sets Tiffany apart is not just her personal journey, but the unwavering commitment she has to lifting others. Despite grappling with her own heartache, she remains a steadfast nurturer, embodying love and sisterhood in all her interactions. I have seen her step onto the front lines, offering encouraging words and a listening ear to those in need—reminding us all that we are never truly alone in our struggles. Her dedication to doing God's work is profoundly inspiring; she brings healing to countless women, including myself, through her compassionate spirit and wise counsel.

I remember the first time I sat in her office, carrying the weight of the world on my shoulders—terrified, broken, and unloved. And there was Tiffany, with her bright smile and an open heart, seeing beauty in my brokenness when I could not. She helped me understand that when a heart breaks, it opens itself to the possibility of more love, healing, and renewal. Her encouragement planted seeds of hope in me, and I will forever be grateful for the profound impact she has had on my life.

In the pages of this book, you will discover Tiffany's unwavering faith, her insights on healing, and the love that flows from her heart. Her words are a balm for the weary soul, offering reassurance that indeed —it's gonna be alright. As you embark on this journey with her, may you find strength, inspiration, and the courage to rise above your own challenges.

I am truly thankful to know such an extraordinary woman—a true angel on earth. Thank you, Tiffany, for your relentless spirit, your nurturing heart, and your unwavering faith.

Your influence is a gift to us all.

PREFACE

This book was born from a place of deep pain, but also deep purpose.

For years, I lived in silence. I was the strong one. The accomplished one. The woman who wore every hat, carried every burden, and kept smiling through it all. From the outside, I had it together: degrees, a successful career, a beautiful family. But inside, I was unraveling.

Like so many women, I was trapped in generational cycles I didn't yet have words for—repeating the unspoken patterns of the women before me. My inner child was still aching, still unseen. I didn't know how to set emotional boundaries. I didn't understand the spiritual battle I was in. And yet, I kept surviving. Until one day, survival wasn't enough. That's where this book begins.

There were no broken bones—just the slow erosion of my self-worth. I wrote *It's Gonna Be Alright* because I know I'm not alone. There are so many women like me; women who are high-functioning, successful, and respected, yet suffering quietly in emotionally toxic relationships. Women who doubt their instincts because the pain isn't visible to others. Women who feel guilty for wanting more, for choosing themselves, for saying "enough."

This book is my truth. It's my healing journey, written with raw honesty and an open heart. It's for the woman who feels confused, afraid, exhausted, and yet still shows up. It's for the woman who thinks she's the only one questioning her sanity. It's for the woman who is finally ready to stop shrinking, to stop explaining, and to start healing.

I didn't write this as a therapist; I wrote this as a woman. A woman who finally found the strength to break the cycle. A woman who rediscovered her voice. A woman who surrendered her healing to God and trusted Him to carry her through.

If you're holding this book, I want you to know: you are seen. You are not crazy. You are not alone. You are worthy of peace, of healing, of love that doesn't come with pain.

And I promise you… *it's gonna be alright.*

WHO IS TIFFANY M. CIVERS?
THE WOMAN BEHIND THE WORDS

By the time this book is in your hands, I will proudly be a grandmother—something that fills me with absolute joy. I am a grandmother to a beautiful grandson, a mother of three incredible adult children, and a woman who has lived, learned, broken, healed, and risen.

I've spent over two decades serving the Harlem community as a school psychologist, writing psychological evaluations and IEPs—especially for minority students whose stories are often overlooked. I am also a licensed therapist and the founder, CEO, and lead clinician at *It's Never Too Late Mental Health Counseling, PLLC*. While I manage the day-to-day operations of the practice, I still provide therapy because I genuinely love what I do. Helping others is not just my profession—it is my calling.

I'm not the one-way therapist. If my client is struggling with vocational goals, we talk about that. If it's parenting, relationships, or trauma—we talk about that too. I meet people where they are, help them bypass the hoops and roadblocks, and pour into them with everything I have. My work is layered because life is layered.

I am a survivor of an emotionally toxic life. A woman who wakes up every morning and chooses herself—even on the hard days. I experience joy and freedom in ways I never thought possible. My past no longer defines me—it refined me.

I love God with my whole heart. I know without a doubt that I wouldn't be here without Him. Through all my mistakes, He waited. He protected me. He reminded me that I was always His. I thank God for loving me back to life.

I am a woman of color. A woman of perseverance, strength, self-respect, and dignity. A woman who loves herself deeply, who has standards, who knows her worth, and who knows how she deserves to be loved. And though emotions may come and old habits may try to creep in, I know who I am now.

I'm proud of how far I've come. I'm proud of how much I've survived. And most of all, I'm happy for me. Truly happy. That wasn't always the case—but now, I am content. I'm finally living a life I chose on my terms.

Motherhood is one of my greatest honors. Being a young mother came with mistakes, but I've worked tirelessly to break generational cycles with my children. I listen. I apologize. I accept. I support. I validate. I create space for honesty. And when I fall short, I'm open to doing better.

To every woman reading this:
I will forever be you, and you will forever be me.

There are so many similarities—some obvious, some quiet—but foundations are foundations. And at some point, we realize how much of our stories overlap. The details may differ, but the pain, the survival, the desire to be seen? That's universal.

I want to be remembered as the woman who looked just like you…

- The woman who learned to compartmentalize her pain and still got things done
- The woman who achieved success while silently hurting
- The woman who struggled—and still showed up
- The woman who pushed through

I am the first person in my family to graduate. And that means something. Behind every degree, every title, every step I've taken— there was a little girl carrying the weight of everything she never said. And still, she rose.

And I am a book writer. A woman who courageously chronicled her life—bit by bit, step by step—and poured gallons of tears into these pages. I was brave enough, vulnerable enough, to share the deep, dark secrets of my life—even knowing many wouldn't understand it, accept it, or might even question it.

But I wrote it anyway. I did it!

It took courage. It took strength. It took a level of honesty I had once been afraid to give. And with every word, every chapter, came healing. Writing this book was not just a creative act—it was an act of survival. It was a reclaiming. It was liberation.

So, if you see yourself in these pages, know this: I see you too. We are not so different.

And no matter what brought you here, I promise— *it's gonna be alright!*

INTRODUCTION

This book is not just a story—it's a journey through pain, healing, and reclaiming my power.

Although I am a Licensed Mental Health Counselor, a School Psychologist, and hold multiple certifications, this book is not written from the lens of a clinician. It is written from the raw, unfiltered perspective of a woman who endured psychological distress, manipulation, and gaslighting.

This is a story for the women who feel unseen, unheard, and trapped in a cycle they can't put into words. Women who don't realize they're carrying decades of generational trauma in their bones. Women who wonder why setting boundaries feels like betrayal. Women who sense a spiritual heaviness they can't explain—but deeply feel.

For years, I didn't have the words either. I just knew the weight of what I carried, the exhaustion of fighting to be understood, and the silent grief of mourning a relationship that was never what I believed it to be.

This book is not a therapy guide. It is a testament to survival, to breaking free, and to knowing that healing is possible. It is written in a format that reflects the healing process itself: raw emotions intertwined with the events that shaped them. Some days are full of clarity. Some are clouded by pain. And others are small victories where the light starts to shine through.

If you've ever...

- Questioned yourself because someone convinced you that you were the problem...
- Felt alone in your pain...
- Wondered if it's even possible to start over...

.

This book is for you.

.

Because no matter what you've been through—
it's gonna be alright.

PART ONE
THE BREAKING

Before healing begins, there is the breaking. The unraveling. The silent suffering behind closed doors.

This section reveals the early wounds, inherited patterns, and deep emotional trauma that shaped how I saw love, myself, and survival. These are the moments that cracked me open—but also began to reveal the parts of me that needed to be rebuilt.

If you find yourself here, know this: it's okay to not be okay.

This is where truth begins.

CHAPTER 1
THE FOUNDATION

Vulnerability. That's where this all began.

When I reflect on the foundation of my life—not the life people see now, but the real one—it began with pain, survival, and inherited patterns. It began in the moments I watched my mother make decisions not from wholeness, but from heartbreak. A young widow with three small children, trying to navigate a life that had imploded. She was doing what she could. But what she could do came at a cost—to her and to us.

She chose a partner who wasn't a father figure. He wasn't kind, he wasn't loving, and he didn't care to build any relationship with us. I remember a two-year stretch where he and I didn't speak. Not a word. And my mother allowed it. That silence should have been addressed. But it was normalized.

That's what dysfunction does—it trains you to live with the unacceptable. Some people grow up and break every generational curse they came from. Others find themselves repeating it—unintentionally, subconsciously, but with precision. I fell into the latter. Even though I promised myself I wouldn't.

I remember the exact moment I decided to let my emotionally toxic partner move in with me. It was impulsive. It was driven by fear. And it was rooted in the same kind of vulnerability I had watched my mother move from all those years before.

He told me his parole officer was threatening to violate him, and that he needed to move immediately. I was newly out of a relationship, emotionally raw, and still healing. My children were young. I didn't stop to think about the long-term effects—on me, on him, on our stability. I just wanted to take care of him. I wanted to save him.

So, after three months of dating, I let him move in. My justification? I've known him for four years! But, what I ignored was the glaring truth: this man was on lifetime parole.

Here I was—a young mother of two, fresh out of college, trying to set a strong foundation for my kids. And I opened the door to a man who wasn't in a position to lead, provide, or protect. I pushed my own needs to the side. My children's stability became secondary. And for what? A sense of connection? A temporary partner in transition?

That was the beginning of me consistently putting myself and my children on the back burner in order to hold space for my boyfriend's healing—someone who wasn't even showing up whole for himself.

Twenty years of marriage later, when the dust started to settle, I realized something: I had become my mother.

She let someone into our lives who couldn't offer emotional safety or security, and now I had done the same. I wasn't thinking, "Can this man provide for us? Does he have what it takes to pour into our family?" I never saw a provider growing up, so I didn't look for one.

All I thought was: "How can I help him?"

And when the discomfort started, I rationalized it the same way I had seen her do. I told myself, "Well, my children have their biological father. He can just be here for me. He doesn't need to be their father." But, that logic was flawed. I was compartmentalizing dysfunction— trying to keep it in its own little corner while pretending it wouldn't spread.

Later in life, that realization gave me compassion. For my mom. For myself. I understood her choices because I had made them too. We do so much subconsciously, repeating what we saw, not realizing how deeply ingrained those patterns are—until one day, we look up and say: "Wow, I became her." The only difference was, I thought I was breaking the cycle.

I told myself, "I'll never let a man mistreat my kids. If he yells at them or talks down to them, I'm done." That was the promise I made to myself. And I kept it. But, I didn't realize that harm isn't always loud. Sometimes, it's in what you allow, in what you excuse, in what you normalize behind closed doors.

I thought I was exempt because I was conscious. Because I knew better. But, knowing isn't the same as doing better. And intention isn't the same as healing.

So, yes, this is where the foundation was laid—in broken patterns, in inherited choices, in silence and shame and survival.

But, that isn't where it ends.

Because once I saw it clearly—once I understood the cycle—I made the choice to build something different.

To break what had broken me.

To create what I had never seen.

This is where the healing began.

* * *

YOUR TURN TO HEAL

1. What patterns from your childhood or family history have shown up in your relationships today?

_____

_____

_____

_____

_____

_____

_____

_____

_____

_____

2. Have you ever ignored a red flag out of fear, hope, or a desire to save someone else?

_____

_____

_____

_____

_____

_____

_____

_____

_____

_____

RAW EMOTIONS

Take a moment to reflect on what this chapter stirred in you. Use the space below to write out any raw, unfiltered emotions that surfaced— no judgment, just honesty. Sometimes the act of naming what you feel is the first step toward healing.

_____

_____

_____

_____

_____

_____

_____

_____

_____

_____

_____

_____

_____

CHAPTER 2
THE DAY I LEARNED TO DISAPPEAR

I remember the day my father died.

To understand the weight of that moment, you'd need to know a little about him. My father struggled with addiction—he was both an alcoholic and a heroin user. But as a child, I didn't fully understand what that meant. What I did know was that he was present. He was the parent who was home. He took us out, spent time with us, and gave us his attention.

Despite his addictions, I didn't see him as an addict—I saw him as my dad.

He was in a car accident when we were young—hit by a truck. Because of that accident, he received a settlement—hundreds of thousands of dollars. He walked with a limp, drove a Jeep Cherokee, and always dressed sharp. The finest clothes. The flyest gear. He made sure we looked just as good, too.

I remember him buying my mom a beautiful pair of alligator shoes and always wanting her to dress nice. He took pride in his appearance, and he took pride in us.

He'd sing to us as he got us dressed. I can still hear him say,

"Mirror, mirror on the wall, who is the prettiest of them all?"

And I'd proudly answer, "I am!"

And without missing a beat, he'd say, "You sure are."

He told me I was beautiful. Smart. Talented. He told me why my name was Tiffany. He gave me identity. He saw me. He celebrated me.

He would take us out and show us off: "Look at my girls. Sing for me. Dance for me." And we would. We were the stars in his sky. I felt like a princess in a castle. He made me feel like my little nothings—my songs, my silly dances—were magic.

Those memories are so vivid, so full of light, that it was hard for me to recognize his struggle. As a child, I didn't see the effects of his addiction. I didn't see poverty. I didn't see him begging for money or falling apart. Because, sadly, he had the means to fund his addiction. So, while my mother may have seen the darker side of his reality, I saw the man who made me feel special.

And that's something we don't talk about enough—how two people in the same house can experience the same person in completely different ways. My father may have been toxic to my mother, but he was tender to me.

That duality shaped me more than I ever realized. I had a version of him that felt safe, adored, and seen.

And that's the version I grieved when he died.

My father was incarcerated for about a year. By the time he came home, he was ill. I remember sitting on the couch, looking at him, thinking, *Who is this man?* I felt so disconnected. Not long after, he passed away from cirrhosis of the liver. Alcohol had damaged him from the inside out, but as a child, I couldn't understand that.

I just knew he was gone.

That day is burned into my memory. The house was full of family, and everyone was talking to my mom. I trailed behind her like a little shadow, watching her every move, waiting to see if she would cry, so I could know how to feel.

But, she didn't. And eventually, she turned to me and said, "Tiffany, stop following me. I'm okay."

I just looked at her and said, "I just wanted to make sure you were okay."

Even at six years old, I had learned to silence my own pain in order to tend to someone else's.

That was the beginning of my codependency—before I even knew what that word meant.

My emotions didn't matter. My grief didn't matter.

The message was clear: Be okay.

Make sure others are okay.

And I carried that with me.

When I was thirteen, I lost someone else—my boyfriend.

He was five years older than me, and I wasn't supposed to be dating him. My mother had warned me, *Don't see him,* but I didn't listen.

He was involved in street life—controlling, verbally aggressive. I didn't understand why he had to be so mean to me when I tried so hard to listen, to please him.

But, now I see that relationship mirrored what I experienced at home with my siblings.

We all had responsibilities, but the weight of them often fell on me. There was one sibling in particular who would flat-out refuse to help—refuse to do anything. I'd hear, "I'm not doing it. I don't care. You have to."

And just like that, it became my job.

I was the one taking my little sister to daycare, picking her up, starting dinner, making sure things got done. It wasn't fair, but it became normal. I learned to absorb responsibility without questioning it. I became the fixer, the doer, the one who made sure everything kept running—even when it meant silencing my own needs.

That early conditioning taught me to accept imbalance. To stay in situations where control felt familiar. And when someone loved me through control, I didn't always recognize it as unhealthy—because it was what I had always known.

So, when my boyfriend died, I grieved him, too.

Even though he wasn't kind.

Even though I couldn't cry about it at home.

I remember going outside and playing "Baby Hold On to Me" by Gerald Levert and sobbing—finally releasing what I couldn't show anyone else.

I had to cry in secret.

Because I had learned not to make noise with my pain.

I had learned to soothe myself. To stay small. To hold it all in.

And yet, despite it all, there was still this hunger inside me to be seen. To be told I was beautiful, smart, worthy. That part came from my father. The little girl in me who was once twirled around and celebrated never stopped searching for that feeling. That validation. That love.

It's wild how you don't even realize you're in survival mode until you're out of it. But the beauty in all of this—the one gift that pain has offered—is clarity.

When you look back long enough and deep enough, the why becomes clear.

You start to understand where your patterns came from.

The foundation is always there, waiting to be unearthed.

What's not always there is the how.

How do you recover?

How do you unlearn the silence and start to honor your voice?

That's why I wrote this book.

I hope somewhere in these pages, you begin to see your how—

Because no matter what your foundation looked like…

it's gonna be alright.

* * *

YOUR TURN TO HEAL

1. What early memories shaped the way you see yourself today—and how have they influenced the way you show up in relationships?

_____

_____

_____

_____

_____

_____

_____

_____

_____

_____

_____

_____

_____

_____

_____

_____

_____

_____

_____

2. Have you ever silenced your pain to take care of someone else? What would it look like to finally give yourself permission to feel and be seen?

_____

_____

_____

_____

_____

_____

_____

_____

_____

_____

_____

_____

_____

_____

_____

_____

_____

_____

_____

RAW EMOTIONS

Let the little version of you speak here. What did this chapter awaken in your memory, in your heart, in your body? Don't hold back—write freely, without editing or explaining. Sometimes, our youngest wounds just need a safe place to be seen.

_____

_____

_____

_____

_____

_____

_____

_____

_____

_____

_____

_____

_____

_____

_____

_____

_____

_____

_____

_____

_____

_____

_____

_____

_____

_____

_____

CHAPTER 3
HEALING MY INNER CHILD

For years, I didn't realize how deeply my childhood had shaped my patterns. I grew up surrounded by dysfunctional relationship dynamics, and without even knowing it, I internalized it as normal. I wasn't given the emotional security every child deserves. After losing my father at a young age, I learned to prioritize survival over love, safety over fulfillment, and endurance over joy.

I carried emotional burdens that never belonged to me. The words spoken by a family member cut deep—labels like *ugly, stupid,* and *dumb* etched into my self-worth. I was told my lips were too big, my butt too large. At just 13, grieving the sudden death of my boyfriend, I was met not with comfort, but cruelty: "You're cursed," she said. "All your boyfriends will die."

The harshness always followed a simple act of defiance—saying no, choosing myself, standing up when no one else would. That's when the punishment would come: sharp words, cold silence, aggression.

I learned to avoid conflict, to shrink myself, to disappear into books and quiet corners. I believed that surrendering to others' needs was the only way to be treated with any kindness. But the moment I dared to say no, to hold a boundary, I was met with rage and rejection.

As I grew into womanhood, the mistreatment only deepened.

I remember walking out of a hair salon one day, the rain pouring. This close family member demanded my umbrella. I asked if we could share since I had just gotten my hair done, but she refused.

"All or nothing," she said. Then she jumped in a cab, leaving me to walk home in the rain.

I couldn't understand how someone could treat me like that. Over time, it started to feel normal—until it didn't.

Her kindness was always conditional. When I complied, she was sweet, even affectionate. But the moment I chose myself, I was met with resentment, emotional withdrawal, or outright cruelty. My accomplishments were never celebrated—only criticized.

I remember going to a party one night with friends. It was my first time drinking Hennessy. I didn't realize how strong it was. I took five shots and quickly became overwhelmed. I didn't know my limit.

I asked her to walk me to the car. At first, she said no, then finally agreed—in her usual annoyed tone. She brought me to the car and told me to stay put. I begged her to take me home, but she refused.

"I'm not leaving the party because of you," she said.

I pleaded with her not to leave the car door open, telling her I couldn't feel my body and was terrified something bad would happen. She ignored me and walked away. Thankfully, a friend took pity and drove me home.

That night made something painfully clear:

There was no love.

No compassion.

No care.

Just hatred dressed up as this close family member.

And that's when I discovered: I wasn't safe. Not with her. Not even in a crisis.

From that moment on, I knew—no one was coming to save me.

I had to protect myself.

I had to become my own safe place.

And through all of this—years of unkind words, of bread-crumbed affection, of emotional neglect and mistreatment—I never, ever received an apology. Not once.

I was always made to feel like this treatment was just a part of life, something I had to accept. But never did she say, "I'm sorry." So, apologies became something foreign to me—something I didn't know, something I never received. And that absence left a scar, teaching me to expect pain without acknowledgment, hurt without healing.

Looking back, I see that I wasn't just surviving—I was enduring. And that endurance shaped me. I became the one who showed up, who carried the weight, who kept going without complaint. But in learning how to show up for everyone else, I never learned how to show up for myself.

When I finally began to heal, I had to face the little girl inside me— the one who never felt seen, who was forced to be strong, to silence her feelings, to survive without a safety net.

I sat with her. I imagined holding her, looking into her eyes, and saying all the things she should've heard back then:

You are worthy.
You are enough.
You are loved.

I waited for years—for an apology, for someone to rescue me, for someone to say, "You deserved better."

But, that moment never came. So, I gave it to myself. And now I know: *I am the one I've been waiting for.*

* * *

YOUR TURN TO HEAL

1. What messages or memories from your childhood still live in your body or self-talk today?

_____

_____

_____

_____

_____

_____
_____
_____
_____

2. If you could speak to your younger self, what truths would you want her to hear?

_____
_____
_____
_____
_____
_____
_____
_____
_____

RAW EMOTIONS

Take a moment to write to the little girl inside you. What did this chapter stir in her? Let your pen hold space for the memories, the ache, the hope. You don't need to fix or explain anything—just be with whatever rises, gently and truthfully.

_____
_____
_____
_____
_____
_____
_____
_____
_____
_____

CHAPTER 4
THE AWAKENING

I t didn't happen in therapy or during a fight. It happened in a store, under bright lights, holding something I didn't need—when I realized I couldn't keep living the life I was barely surviving.

It wasn't dramatic. It wasn't a grand, life-altering event. It was subtle. Quiet. Just me, standing in Saks Fifth Avenue on a Friday evening, staring at something I had convinced myself I needed.

Then it hit me: "Am I going to relive the last twenty years of my life?" The weight of that question nearly brought me to my knees.

For the first time in a long time, I truly saw myself.

The exhaustion in my eyes.

The deep, unshakable sadness I had been carrying for years.

The way I had slowly drifted further away from the person I used to be—all in an effort to maintain something I had convinced myself was worth holding onto.

I had spent years trying to make sense of things that didn't make sense to me. I told myself that if I just tried harder, if I just endured a little longer, if I just poured more love into the situation, things would change. But, they didn't.

I finally had to face the truth.

I was losing myself.

I couldn't remember what made me laugh.

What I liked.

What I needed.

My voice had become so entangled in survival, I forgot how to use it. For so long, I believed that love meant sacrifice. That strength meant endurance. That if I could just outlast the pain, eventually, joy would follow.

But, in that moment, standing in a department store, I realized something profound: I was never meant to just survive. I was meant to live. And yet—I wasn't living.

I had been so focused on avoiding conflict, keeping the peace, and maintaining expectations that I had silenced my own needs. My identity had become intertwined with making things work, even at the cost of my own happiness.

Healing meant taking accountability not just for the ways I had been hurt, but for the ways I had neglected myself. It meant acknowledging that somewhere along the way, I had stopped advocating for my own joy.

I thought about the weight of this realization—not just for myself, but for my children. For my sense of self-worth. For the way I showed up in the world.

I had to sit with the uncomfortable truth that I had spent years prioritizing everything, but myself. But, here's the beautiful thing about awakening: It's never too late. As I stood there, I felt something shift inside me.

I didn't have all the answers.

I didn't know what the journey ahead would look like.

I didn't have a roadmap.

I didn't know where it would lead.

But, I knew this: I was done abandoning myself. And for the first time in a long time, I wasn't begging to be chosen. I was choosing me.

* * *

YOUR TURN TO HEAL

1. What was your personal "awakening" moment—the shift where you started to see your worth?

_____

_____

_____

_____

_____

_____

_____

_____

_____

_____

_____

_____

_____

2. What parts of yourself have you silenced in the name of keeping the peace?

_____

_____

_____

_____

_____

_____

_____

_____

_____

_____

_____

_____

_____

RAW EMOTIONS

Let this be the space where you name the moment it all shifted. Where were you when you realized you couldn't keep living half-alive? Let whatever emotions rise—grief, relief, clarity, or confusion. This is your turning point. Write from the place inside you that finally whispered, "I deserve more."

_____
_____
_____
_____
_____
_____
_____
_____
_____
_____
_____
_____
_____
_____
_____
_____
_____
_____
_____
_____
_____
_____
_____
_____
_____
_____

CHAPTER 5
THE PAIN WAS ALWAYS THERE

Every vacation, my spouse and I argued.

It had become a pattern—one I refused to acknowledge for too long.

This time, however, something was different. The detachment was palpable. It wasn't just in the words, but in the tone, the body language, the way the air between us had shifted.

The calls during my trip became fewer, shorter, obligatory. The concern felt scripted, as if it was more of a task than a genuine check-in. It was as if a decision had already been made, and I was just the last to know.

Then came the comment—simple, yet laced with something I couldn't quite define: "You should extend your vacation."

It wasn't a suggestion; it was a dismissal.

For the first time, I felt a distance that wasn't just physical.

But, as always, I shrugged it off. I pushed away the gnawing feeling, convincing myself that we would recover like we always had. That whatever was happening would pass. That the tension would dissolve once I returned home.

So, when my trip ended, I expected things to fall back into place.

"Hey, are you going to pick me up from the airport?"

"Sure," came the response—flat, indifferent, rehearsed.

And just like that, I let myself believe that everything was fine.

But, it wasn't.

The moment I got in the car from the airport, something felt off. There was no warmth in his greeting. No curious questions about my trip. No sign that my absence had even mattered. Just a routine peck on the cheek, a hollow welcome, and silence.

I told myself I was imagining things. That I was just tired from traveling. That once I unpacked, settled in, and life resumed, everything would feel normal again.

I was wrong.

My son and I had just returned from ten days in Aruba. The moment we stepped inside, his voice cut through the stillness.

"Mom, Mom, Mom! What happened? Did you argue?"

Confused, I turned to him. "What are you talking about?"

His wide eyes flickered with panic. Then, I followed his gaze to the empty closet. He had walked into his bedroom—the closet they had shared—and saw it.

No clothes.

No shoes.

No trace that he had ever lived there.

The closet was stripped bare.

My son's voice cracked. "Is this happening again?" That's when it hit me. This time was different.

Over the years, there had been dramatic fights. Arguments that ended in packed bags, slammed doors, temporary separations. Clothes thrown into suitcases, garbage bags, or storage.

But, this wasn't that.

This wasn't a fight.

This wasn't a threat.

This was final.

He left.

Secretly.

Quietly.

Without a word.

It took me a few days to realize what had happened.

First, the closet.

Then the silence.

Then, the credit card receipt.

And in that moment, the truth settled in my bones. I had ignored the signs for years. But, they had always been there. I just wasn't ready to face them.

The house felt empty.

Silent.

But, the silence wasn't peaceful—it was suffocating.

For days, I wandered through my home, trying to process what had just happened. One moment, we were a family. The next, I was standing in the middle of a war zone, not knowing how I got there.

I couldn't escape the weight of it. Everywhere I turned, I was reminded of his absence.

The space in the closet where his clothes used to be.

The empty spot at the dinner table.

The silence where there was once an argument, a passive-aggressive comment, or even just the sound of his footsteps.

Perhaps the hardest part of all was seeing the pain in my child's eyes. My son and I barely spoke—not because we were angry with each other, but because we didn't know what to say. There were no words that could describe the void we both felt.

To add pain to injury, after he left, I discovered a parking ticket in my car window. When I Googled where it came from, it was from a local hotel in my area.

Did he use my car to take a woman to a hotel?

Why would he use my car when he had his own?

Did he want me to find it?

The questions played in my mind so much, I felt like I was losing it. Like I was going insane.

I discovered through credit card statements that the night at the hotel was also met with my favorite Baumgart meal and a bottle of Patrón—exactly the same way we celebrated. I couldn't believe it.

I thought to myself, "Was he repeating our same life with someone else?"

A few nights after he left, I took my son to Ruth's Chris Steak House, hoping that maybe a change of scenery would help us both.

Maybe if we pretended to be okay, we could find a moment of normalcy.

We barely ate.

We barely talked.

Then, as he pushed his food around his plate, he finally spoke: "Mom, our life was just different a week ago." His voice was quiet, but the pain behind his words was deafening.

I nodded. "I know."

We just sat there, staring at our plates, numb.

At that moment, I realized something: This wasn't just my pain. It was his, too.

For so long, I had convinced myself that staying was for my son. That if I held on, if I kept things together, he wouldn't have to suffer the pain of a broken home. In reality, he had been suffering all along.

Now, he was grieving a life that had already been falling apart for years. Grieving a relationship that was already over.

I had never experienced pain like this before. It wasn't just heart-break. It wasn't just sadness. It was grief.

The kind of grief that lingers in the air.

That makes every breath feel heavier.

That settles in your bones and makes you question everything you thought you knew.

I cried daily. I begged God to take the pain away. "God, please. I can't do this. I can't feel this. Just make it stop." I laid face down on the floor, arms stretched out, sobbing into the silence. The pain wouldn't stop.

And still, I had to get up every morning.

Still had to parent my child.

Still had to go to work, pay the bills, keep moving forward—even when I didn't want to.

This wasn't just about losing a partner. It was about losing the illusion I had clung to for so long. It was about realizing that no matter how much I had given, how much I had fought, how much I had endured—none of it was ever going to be enough.

You see, love shouldn't be something you have to fight for. For years, I fought to be seen, to be loved, to be enough.

But, now I knew: the only love worth fighting for… was my own.

* * *

YOUR TURN TO HEAL

1. Have you ever ignored signs that something was wrong because you weren't ready to face the truth?

_____

_____

_____

_____

_____

_____

_____

_____

_____

_____

2. What unspoken pain have you been carrying that others may not see?

_____

_____

_____

_____

_____

_____

_____

_____

_____

_____

RAW EMOTIONS

Sometimes the deepest pain isn't in what was said—it's in what was left unsaid. In the quiet moments, in the empty spaces, in the things you couldn't make sense of. Let your pen speak what your heart has held. Grieve it. Name it. You don't have to make sense of it. You just have to let it out.

_____

_____

_____

_____

_____

_____

_____

_____

_____

_____

_____

_____

_____

_____

_____

_____

_____

_____

_____

_____

_____

_____

_____

_____

_____

_____

RAW EMOTIONS

A MOMENT OF REFLECTION

As I write these words, I feel so emotional.
Tears are rolling down my face.

I feel vulnerable.
I feel afraid.
I feel like all of the emotions I buried years ago are resurfacing,
pulling me back into moments I thought I had healed from.
I feel alone.
I feel damaged.
I feel like I wasted so much of my life.

There is an ache inside me that I can't explain —
A weight that sits heavy on my chest.
A grief that lingers, whispering all the things I have tried so
hard to let go of.

Even in this moment, as the tears fall, I feel something else.
I feel the presence of God.
I feel His hand holding mine, steadying me, whispering to me
that this is healing.

That this pain I feel now is not meant to break me—
It is meant to release me.
That these words are not just for me,

But for every woman who has suffered in silence.
I am not alone. I never was.
Neither are you.

CHAPTER 6
THE BEGINNING OF THE WAR

While I was grieving the end of our family, he was already lawyering up. He wanted to "settle amicably." But I knew what that really meant. He was rushing a settlement offer to avoid full financial disclosure and lengthy legal proceedings. It wasn't about fairness or co-parenting—it was about securing what he believed he was entitled to, without accountability.

He wanted freedom from responsibility.

He wanted everything I had worked for.

Despite years of promising he'd never touch my pension or retirement, he wanted both.

He wanted half of the money I saved for our son's college tuition.

He wanted a portion of my stock investments.

His debts? Covered.

My assets? On the table.

But, child support? Nowhere in sight.

And any mention of shared custody or our son residing with him part-time? Not a word.

In fact, shortly after leaving, he moved into a studio apartment with a single bed—making overnights or joint physical custody of our sixteen-year-old son impossible. In my opinion, this was never about co-parenting. It was about freedom—freedom from responsibility, from parenting, from anything that tied him to the life he chose to walk away from.

And to add to the betrayal, just one month after he left, he revealed in an email rant that he had already consulted an attorney months before.

So while I was grieving, confused, and trying to keep our home stable, he was quietly planning his exit.

Let's be clear: he left.

In my eyes, he abandoned his family for his own desires and infidelities. He walked away. But, I filed. Not out of revenge—but out of resurrection.

Out of necessity.

Out of the quiet, growing certainty that I deserved to live free.

Once I filed, there was no turning back.

The manipulation, the betrayals, the psychological warfare—it was all coming into the light.

And I still filed.

Because for the first time in my life, I chose me. And in that moment, I knew— I would never lose myself again.

This process was nothing like I expected. Every time I spoke to my attorney, I heard the same phrase over and over: "Tiffany, you're vulnerable." That word *vulnerable* felt like a dagger every time I heard it.

I was vulnerable—not emotionally, but financially—because I made more money. I was the breadwinner. The stable one. I was vulnerable because the system doesn't care about the years of emotional misuse I endured; it only cares about numbers. And in the eyes of the law, that meant I owed him. Now, I was being told that I would have to pay him alimony. The air left my lungs. "God, I can't do this. I can't. After all these years of sacrifice, I have to pay? For the next twenty years?"

I had spent years working long hours, building a life for my family. I put my dreams on hold to make sure everyone else was secure. My attorney tried to convince me to just settle. "It's the best way to move forward," she said. But, I couldn't. I refused.

I was left with all the bills, all the responsibilities. Now I had to pay out? My retirement, the money I had saved, the money I planned for my child's education…

The level of entitlement was indescribable. That moment broke me. Not because I didn't expect it, but because of the sheer audacity of it. There was no guilt, no remorse, no empathy—just entitlement.

That's when I knew: this wasn't just an ending. This was a war.

The settlement offers came next.

Half of everything.

Half of my savings.

Half of my investments.

Half of my future.

Meanwhile, I was left paying all the bills alone. Physically and financially raising a child alone. Holding all the financial responsibilities we created together. Somehow, I obliged.

I dropped to my knees that night, sobbing. "God, this is unfair. This is cruel. I cannot do this." But, I could. God had already told me it would be over in a year.

I didn't know how.

I didn't know when.

But, I held on to that promise with everything I had left.

And the next morning—and every morning thereafter— I got up and fought. I refused to let him take anything else from me.

* * *

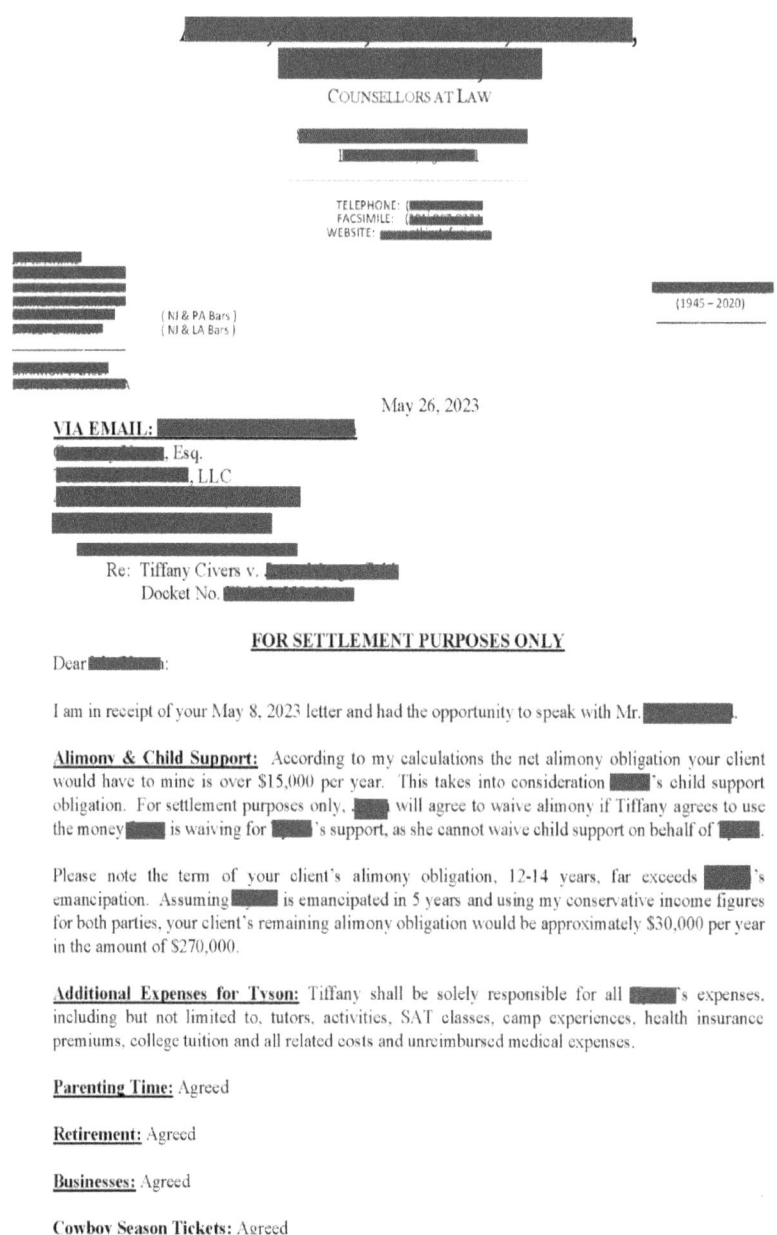

Counsellors at Law

TELEPHONE: ▓
FACSIMILE: ▓
WEBSITE: ▓

(NJ & PA Bars)
(NJ & LA Bars)

(1945 – 2020)

May 26, 2023

VIA EMAIL: ▓
▓, Esq.
▓, LLC
▓
▓

Re: Tiffany Civers v. ▓
Docket No. ▓

FOR SETTLEMENT PURPOSES ONLY

Dear ▓:

I am in receipt of your May 8, 2023 letter and had the opportunity to speak with Mr. ▓.

Alimony & Child Support: According to my calculations the net alimony obligation your client would have to mine is over $15,000 per year. This takes into consideration ▓'s child support obligation. For settlement purposes only, ▓ will agree to waive alimony if Tiffany agrees to use the money ▓ is waiving for ▓'s support, as she cannot waive child support on behalf of ▓.

Please note the term of your client's alimony obligation, 12-14 years, far exceeds ▓'s emancipation. Assuming ▓ is emancipated in 5 years and using my conservative income figures for both parties, your client's remaining alimony obligation would be approximately $30,000 per year in the amount of $270,000.

Additional Expenses for Tyson: Tiffany shall be solely responsible for all ▓'s expenses, including but not limited to, tutors, activities, SAT classes, camp experiences, health insurance premiums, college tuition and all related costs and unreimbursed medical expenses.

Parenting Time: Agreed

Retirement: Agreed

Businesses: Agreed

Cowboy Season Tickets: Agreed

Debt: Agreed

, Esq.
Civers v. ▮▮▮▮▮▮▮
May 25, 2023
Page 2

Counsel Fees: Tiffany to contribute $11,000 toward ▮▮▮▮'s counsel fees.

Funds Owed to ▮▮▮ for Car: Tiffany to pay ▮▮▮ $3,400 which represents the funds ▮▮▮ loaned to Tiffany's son from a prior marriage and paid back to him upon the sale of the vehicle.

Painting: ▮▮▮ has an artist painted picture on the wall in the house he would like returned to him.

In the event we are unable to resolve the matter, Given the disparity in the parties' incomes, I will need to file a *pendente lite* application for support, contribution to ▮▮▮'s counsel fees and payment of the forensic accountant.

This is for settlement purposes only and shall not be submitted to any court or arbitrator without express permission of Mr. ▮▮▮▮▮▮.

Very truly yours,

▮▮▮▮▮▮▮▮▮▮

SLM
cc: ▮▮▮▮▮▮▮▮ (via mail)

YOUR TURN TO HEAL

1. Have you ever had to fight a quiet battle no one else could see—legal, emotional, or spiritual?

_____

_____

_____

_____

_____

_____

_____

_____

_____

_____

_____

_____

_____

_____

_____

_____

_____

2. What is one way you can reclaim your power today, even if someone tried to strip it from you?

_____

_____

_____

_____

_____

_____

_____

_____

_____

_____

_____

_____

_____

_____

_____

_____

_____

_____

_____

_____

_____

_____

_____

RAW EMOTIONS

When everything you built is threatened and the pain feels louder than justice, it's okay to feel anger. It's okay to feel grief. Let yourself release what you were never meant to carry alone. This is your space to scream, to cry, to breathe—and to reclaim your voice in the aftermath of betrayal.

_____

_____

_____

_____

_____

_____

_____

_____

_____

_____

_____

CHAPTER 7
THE TWIST FROM REALITY

I t wasn't just about twisting the truth—it was about erasing my reality, rewriting my story, and making me question everything I knew to be true.

My ex-husband didn't just manipulate words; I felt as if he wanted to manipulate my identity.

It got to the point where he started studying my career. He mirrored my profession, absorbing the language of psychology and mental health. Using clinical terms to describe me, he would say:

"You have childhood wounds."

"You are insecure."

"You sure you weren't sexually abused as a child?"

"You sure you were neglected as a child?"

"You are toxic."

"You are deflecting."

That last one—*you are deflecting*—became his favorite the moment I held him accountable for his actions.

There was so much cognitive dissonance and confusion, I often wondered if I was competent or fit to be a therapist. If I was even worthy of the career I had built with years of education and sacrifice.

He immersed himself in psychology podcasts, read articles,

watched videos, and began calling himself a coach—despite never completing any formal education or certifications. He crafted a persona, one that made him seem insightful, authoritative, even wise.

Meanwhile, I was the one with college degrees, years of experience, and real-world expertise. And somehow, I became the patient in his narrative.

I had encouraged him to finish college and pursue a career as a life coach. I thought I was supporting what he said was his passion in the mental health field. But he never finished college or completed any certification programs, even after starting them.

My ex-husband never congratulated me or praised me for my accomplishments. Instead, over the years, he'd say things like:

"Well, you have a college degree—I don't."

"Why are you spending Sundays away from the kids to do an internship? I have a life also."

So, I decided to focus on his professional growth. I figured if *he* felt successful, maybe he'd feel proud of me, too.

I never put up any of my multiple college degrees or diplomas in our home. I downplayed my success in hopes that it would make him feel more accepting of me.

What I didn't realize at the time was this: I was giving him the tools to further mistreat me. The tactics expanded beyond our private conversations and became public. Later, I learned he had planted seeds of doubt in my family members, my children, and our mutual friends. He was slowly rewriting the story of our relationship.

I later saw social media posts full of veiled insults and vague accusations. The kind meant to discredit without saying a name. The kind meant to wound without accountability.

There is a level of emotional mistreatment people don't see— the slow and calculated breakdown of your self-esteem and your self-worth, by attacking the very things that bring you joy. But, if that was his goal, he failed. Because no matter how much he tried to strip me of my worth, I knew one thing with certainty: God saw everything. "Vengeance is mine," says the Lord.

* * *

YOUR TURN TO HEAL

1. Have you ever been made to question your own reality or identity in a relationship?

_____

_____

_____

_____

_____

_____

_____

_____

_____

_____

_____

2. In what ways have you downplayed your success to make others feel comfortable?

_____

_____

_____

_____

_____

_____

_____

_____

_____

_____

_____

_____

RAW EMOTIONS

This is your space to reclaim your truth. Write down the moments you silenced yourself, the confusion you carried, the identity you fought to hold on to. What they tried to rewrite—God is restoring.

CHAPTER 8
POSTPARTUM NEGLECT

remember when he decided he no longer wanted to live in New York. It was right after I had our son.

Those are the moments you need someone the most—the moments when you're emotionally and physically vulnerable. And that's exactly when he vanished.

He said he needed to start a new life for us in Texas.

He said he couldn't make it here.

That the opportunities were better there.

So, he packed up and left.

Our baby was only two months old. I had three kids, a newborn, and no space to breathe or recover.

I was still bleeding.

Still swollen.

Still aching.

And he was gone.

Six months gone.

He left me with a CD duplication business and told me, "This is for you and the family." So, I ran it. Worked it. Around the clock.

I called my cousin to help nanny the kids. I juggled a newborn, my older children, work, the business, and the loneliness that postpartum brings.

Six months of me doing it all.

Six months of survival.

Six months of exhaustion.

He got an apartment in Texas. Lived alone. Started his new life while I stayed behind, holding everything together with my bare hands.

There was no consideration for what I was going through. No regard for my postpartum body, my mind, or my emotional state.

But, I kept going.

Because I had to.

I would whisper to myself, "You cannot be depressed. Shake it off, Tiffany."

If I slipped into darkness, who would take care of my kids? There was no one coming to save me.

I traveled to Texas three times during those six months.

Trying.

Hoping.

Believing his words—that this was for us.

But, every time I showed up, he seemed indifferent to me.

There was nothing to connect us.

No intimacy.

No warmth.

I brought our son so they could bond, but I felt like an invisible presence in the room. I started feeling that familiar ache again—that deep knowing that something wasn't right.

So, I checked the call logs. He had been speaking to another woman every single day. And when I called her, she told me the truth. She didn't even know he was married.

And I stood there—milk-stained, sleep-deprived, and invisible—learning I was sharing the man I was married to with someone who had no idea I existed.

And there I was.

Six months postpartum.

Drained.

Working full time.

Raising our children.

Running his business.

Driving an hour to and from work with an infant in the backseat.

He had left me a business, yes. But— also a burden. I had to produce to survive. He had gone off to Texas to "build for us" while he was living a double life.

When the business hit its lows and started falling apart, he blamed it on the economy.

Blamed it on the recession.

Blamed it on me.

When things fell apart, he seemed to need someone to point at. And I was always the easiest target. It wasn't until I went back and read the emails that I saw it clearly—all the pleading, all the begging.

Asking him to check in.

Asking him to ask me how I was doing.

Asking him to care.

To see me.

And he got angry at my asks.

As if I was asking for too much.

As if needing emotional support made me weak or incapable.

And I had to ask myself: why was I begging someone to care about me? Why was I so desperate? So low?

The truth is this— I had been gaslighting myself. I didn't want to see what was right in front of me. I didn't want to believe that he abandoned me when I needed him most. I didn't want to face the reality that I was in a marriage where my needs didn't matter. I convinced myself that this was what wives were supposed to do.

That sacrifice was part of love.

That struggle was normal.

That he would eventually see me.

But, he never did.

Even after I gave birth.

Even through postpartum.

Even as I carried his child.

I was still the one flying to see him.

He never visited home.

Looking back, I realize how empty I was. How invalidated I felt. How God protected me during a time when I should have broken. Because if it weren't for God, I might not have made it through.

I might have collapsed from exhaustion.

I might have slipped into depression so deep I couldn't return.

But, God kept me!

When no one else saw me, He kept me.

Through the long nights.

Through the exhaustion.

Through the tears.

Through the prayers I was too tired to pray.

He carried me when I had nothing left. And for that, I'm grateful.

Sometimes you don't see the rescue until you look back. Sometimes survival doesn't feel like victory. But, I see now that God didn't let me go.

He held me through the pain.

He held me through the gaslight.

He held me when I was convinced I wasn't enough.

I thank God for keeping me when I could not keep myself!

* * *

YOUR TURN TO HEAL

1. What is one season in your life when you felt unseen or abandoned during a time you needed support?

_____

_____

_____

_____

_____

_____

_____

_____
_____
_____
_____
_____
_____
_____
_____
_____
_____
_____

2. Have you ever convinced yourself that neglect was love? What would you say to that version of yourself now?

_____
_____
_____
_____
_____
_____
_____
_____
_____
_____
_____
_____
_____
_____
_____
_____
_____
_____

RAW EMOTIONS

Let your honesty rise here. If you've ever felt invisible while carrying the weight of the world, this is your space to name it. Your tears matter. Your voice matters. Your truth matters.

_____

_____

_____

_____

_____

_____

_____

_____

_____

_____

_____

_____

_____

_____

_____

_____

_____

_____

_____

_____

_____

_____

_____

_____

_____

_____

_____

_____

RAW EMOTIONS
THE FIGHT CHOSE ME

I often wonder why my life wasn't easier.

Why couldn't I just be raised in peace, grow up happy, go
through normal disappointments, and live a regular life?
Why was my life built around survival?
Why did everything have to be so hard?
Why did I have to be the one to break the cycle?
Why didn't I give up?

I could have.
I'm grown.
I have my own job.
I could be quiet.
I don't have to write this book.
I could disappear from the noise, limit my circle, and spend the
rest of my life in peace.

But, something in me refuses to back down.
Because I know my healing is bigger than me.

This isn't just about my life.
This is about the lives of the women I help.
The children watching me.
The future generations coming after me.

When you're chosen to break a generational curse, the weight is
*   heavy.*
It's exhausting.
But, it's not optional.
It's purpose.

And truthfully, I've watched people who went through the
*   same things I did stay silent.*
Not because they didn't hurt, too.
But because silence is safer.

Speaking up means accountability.
Speaking up means remembering.
Not everyone wants to do that work.
But, I was built for it.
I was called to do it.

If I'm honest, if I knew healing would require this much
*   emotional labor, I probably would've chosen something else.*
But, I didn't know.
And now that I do,
I still choose to stay in the fight.

So, if you're reading this and you're tired, just know this:
You're not alone.
You were chosen, too.

And with that comes the power to shift everything.

Even when it's easier to be quiet.
Even when it feels safer to disappear.

Get back up.

*Fight for your healing like you fight for everything else in your
     life.*

Fight like it matters—because it does.

If you don't fight, someone else will have to start over.

Let the cycle end with you.

PART TWO
THE AWAKENING

Awakening doesn't happen all at once. It comes in waves—small moments of clarity where you begin to question the pain you've normalized.

This section reflects the messy middle: the in-between where you're learning to name what's been hurting you, reclaim what you've lost, and slowly start choosing yourself. It's hard. It's honest. If you're waking up to what no longer serves you, you're on the right path.

This is the beginning of real transformation.

CHAPTER 9
RECLAIMING MYSELF

For a long time, I carried shame like a weight I was never meant to bear. Unfaithful behavior was never something I imagined would be a part of my story. But it was, and I had to face it.

I had a seven-month affair that, in a strange and almost cruel twist, felt like it saved my life. And yet, it became the very weapon that was used to destroy me. I didn't seek it out. I wasn't looking for love or attention. I was drowning in the suffocating grip of an emotionally toxic relationship—feeling invisible, unheard, and completely devalued. I had been manipulated and lied to for so long I questioned my own reality. Then, one day, someone saw me. They acknowledged my presence. They made me feel like I existed again. And for the first time in years, I felt something other than pain.

At that time, my partner and I had already agreed to separate. The plan was set in motion. We were finally going to end the cycle. But then life happened; an unexpected medical issue arose.

And just like that, my freedom was delayed. He refused to leave. He needed time to "figure things out." So, I stayed in a house that felt more like a trap than a home. Days bled into each other. I lived in a home where anger dripped from the walls, where silence screamed louder than words. The resentment was thick, and his calculated coldness stung more than any insult could. I was a prisoner in my own house. I remember the exact moment I felt I had nothing left. I had spent years believing that if I just tried harder, loved deeper, endured longer, maybe he would finally see me. But the truth was, I had disappeared. The woman I once was—the one who believed in love, who believed in herself—was fading fast.

That's when it happened.

The affair wasn't about lust or betrayal—it was about survival. It was like finally coming up for air after nearly drowning. A moment of clarity in the middle of a carefully constructed illusion.

Day after day, while he recovered from his injury, he barely acknowledged me. He slept on the couch. He spent hours on the phone, laughing and talking to others, yet offered me silence. He wasn't working, he wasn't helping around the house, and he never checked in—not even when I was coming home late after closing the office.

When I asked him questions, he gave one-word answers. When I suggested he stay at a family member's home during his recovery, he refused—insisting he was entitled to remain until he got back on his feet. It seemed that I was invisible—single parenting while living with someone who contributed nothing but used everything.

There was a constant tension in the air. He carried himself like someone whose plans had been derailed, as if the only reason he was still in the house was because his injury had delayed his exit. It gave the impression that I was merely a placeholder, not a partner.

And in that atmosphere—where silence felt strategic and presence felt transactional—I started to question everything. I couldn't prove what he was doing, but it felt calculated. It felt like I was being emotionally sidelined while he restructured his life in secret. That's the kind of subterfuge that breaks you down quietly.

For a short time, someone else saw me. Heard me. Considered me. I remembered what it felt like to matter. But, the truth? I wasn't healed. I wasn't ready. I didn't even know how to love myself yet.

That man wasn't my salvation—he was a mirror, reflecting back what I had long forgotten I deserved.

Eventually, I walked away. Cold turkey. No second thoughts. No looking back.

A year later, my ex found out about the affair—not because I confessed, but because he dug. And he weaponized it immediately. After years of his own infidelities, years of my forgiveness, he must have been thrilled to find something to hold over me.

He found old text messages in my phone. Then he checked the computer and saw a canceled trip reservation in someone else's name. That was all it took. Suddenly, I was the villain. Every moment of joy I tried to experience outside of him—vacations, birthdays, promotions—was met with shame and suspicion. He demanded details. Sent group texts to my family, exposing me. Humiliated me. Dismantled any sliver of dignity I had left.

And then he hit me.

I remember it as if it was yesterday. I was lying in bed, half-asleep, when he stormed in with his accusations. "You did this! You're dating him!" I tried to explain, but nothing I said could de-escalate him. His mind was already made up. His pride was already shattered. I turned over and just like that, he punched me. Right in my eye. A full, hard blow while I was still under the covers.

Blood gushed everywhere. The shock numbed me more than the pain. I couldn't process what had just happened. I didn't even know if I'd been hit with something. It was that bad. I remember thinking, "He's never hit me before." But this time, I sensed rage and hatred behind his hand.

I ran into my son's room. Screaming. Crying. My face split open, blood everywhere. I couldn't believe it had happened. My son, in high school, now had to witness this horror. And what did I do? I protected him. I protected my son. And, tragically, I also protected my abuser.

I got in my car and drove myself alone to the hospital in New York. I told the ER staff a lie: that I hit my face on the bedpost. The wound was so bad, I needed surgery. Ten stitches. A black eye. A scar that almost took my vision.

And still, the man I once called my husband— the one I believed would always protect me, love me, and never harm me— stayed home. Checked in once or twice. Told his family. Not one of them asked me if

I was okay. They only wanted to know if I'd called the police. This made me feel so invaluable. Like once again, the priorities were placed on him instead of my well-being.

I came back home with a stitched-up eye and a broken spirit. He apologized, but every "sorry" came with a caveat.

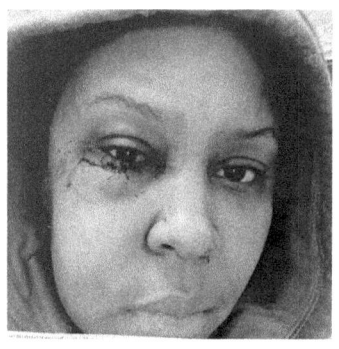

"But you shouldn't have cheated."

"But any man would have reacted that way."

"But I only hit you once."

"But you're trying to make me the monster."

And that's when it struck me.

The abuse that had always been emotional, verbal, psychological was now visible. My pain had finally spilled out onto my face. My face was now the canvas for his rage. And yet, I kept protecting him. Kept trying to convince myself that I caused this.

Because that's what battered women do.

We absorb blame that doesn't belong to us.

We justify the unjustifiable.

We heal ourselves in silence.

I used face masks to hide the swelling. I made excuses. And little by little, my eye began to heal. The physical scars faded. But the emotional ones—the ones no one could see—those took longer. Much longer.

I remember standing in the mirror one day, a year later, barely able to recognize the woman staring back at me. The scar was gone. But, I had changed. God had physically healed me. Restored me. Yet, I still blamed myself. That was the worst part. I believed what my ex-husband believed.

But— no more.

I am human.

I am not my mistake.

I am not anyone's scapegoat.

I am a woman who fought like hell for a relationship that felt like it was destroying her.

A woman who forgave, who endured, who lost herself and clawed her way back.

A woman who reached for comfort in the wrong place and then let it go.

If you've ever made a mistake you thought defined you, hear me now: it does not.

You are not your worst moment.

You are not the lie they tell about you.

You are not their version of the story.

Forgive yourself.

Heal.

Grow.

And do not let anyone—especially someone who wants to punish you—hold your past against you.

You are more than what you've been through.

You are more than what they did.

You are not their guilt.

You are not their projection.

You are God's restoration.

You are more than enough.

* * *

YOUR TURN TO HEAL

1. Have you ever found yourself reaching for something—someone—because you were starving for comfort or connection?

_____

_____

_____

_____

_____

_____
_____
_____
_____

2. What would it look like to forgive yourself for how you coped when you were just trying to survive?

_____
_____
_____
_____
_____
_____
_____

RAW EMOTIONS

There are moments we carry shame for simply trying to survive. If you've ever sought relief in the middle of pain, only to be punished for it later, let this be your space to release the weight. Be gentle with yourself here. Write with honesty, not judgment.

_____
_____
_____
_____
_____
_____
_____
_____
_____
_____
_____
_____

CHAPTER 10
THE BREAKTHROUGH: CHOOSING ME

Breaking free is not just about physically walking away, it's about reclaiming the parts of yourself that you lost along the way. For so long, I had been caught in a cycle of second-guessing, compromising, and shrinking myself to fit into a space that no longer honored who I was. I had convinced myself that if I just endured a little longer, things would change. That if I was patient enough, loving enough, forgiving enough, eventually everything would fall into place. The truth is, healing doesn't come from waiting for someone else to change. It comes from realizing that you deserve more.

There was a moment when I finally understood that I had been waiting for permission to walk away. I had been searching for an undeniable sign, for something that would tell me it was okay to choose myself. But, healing doesn't come wrapped in certainty. It comes in the quiet decision to stop waiting. The permission I was waiting for had to come from me.

Leaving was not easy. It meant facing uncertainty, stepping into the unknown, and rebuilding a life that no longer revolved around trying to fix something that was never mine to fix. It also meant letting go—

not just of the relationship, but of the need to be understood by those who had already made up their minds.

It meant accepting that not everyone would see my heart, not everyone would believe my truth, and not everyone would acknowledge the weight of what I had carried.

For a long time, that hurt. The idea that my pain could be dismissed, that my experiences could be questioned, that my story could be rewritten by those who were never in my shoes. I had to remind myself that healing is not about proving your truth to others. It's about standing in it, regardless of who chooses to believe it. I had spent so much energy holding onto things that drained me, relationships that no longer served me, and narratives that were never mine to carry.

The moment I decided to let go, something inside me shifted. I stopped explaining. I stopped seeking validation. I stopped bearing the weight of other people's expectations. I finally understood something that changed everything: I am enough. Not because someone else says so. Not because I fought to be seen. But because I choose to believe it for myself. Breaking free wasn't just about leaving a situation—it was about stepping into my power. From that moment on, I knew: I would never settle for less than I deserved again.

Letting go was the hardest part of healing. Not just letting go of the relationship, but letting go of the anger, the resentment, the need for closure. For a long time, I wanted him to understand what he had done. I wanted him to feel remorse. I wanted him to acknowledge the pain he had caused.

One day, I realized he never would. I had two choices. I could keep holding onto the pain, replaying the past, waiting for a moment that would never come. Or I could let go and be free. And in choosing freedom, I chose life.

Letting go didn't mean excusing his actions. Letting go didn't mean pretending it didn't hurt. Letting go meant choosing my peace over my pain. It meant releasing myself from the weight of expecting an apology. It meant accepting that justice might never come the way I wanted it to. It meant prioritizing my future over the wounds of my past.

The moment I let go, I felt lighter. Letting go wasn't easy. But it was necessary. I no longer needed to carry my mistakes. I wasn't waiting for validation. I wasn't tied to the version of me that stayed in that cycle. I was finally free.

Free and powerful.

For so long, I had felt powerless. Like I had no control over my own life. Like my happiness was in someone else's hands. Like I was trapped in a cycle I couldn't escape.

The truth is, I had power all along. I had just forgotten how to use it. The moment I decided to emotionally walk away from this marriage, I took back my power. The moment I stopped explaining myself, I took back my power. The moment I realized I didn't need anyone else's permission to be happy, I took back my power.

Reclaiming my power meant learning how to stand up for myself again. It meant setting boundaries and actually enforcing them. It meant saying no without feeling guilty. I started making decisions for myself—not based on fear, not based on what someone else wanted, but based on what was right for me. I found my voice again, and I used it.

I no longer allowed people to take advantage of my kindness. I no longer apologized for being who I was. I no longer accepted less than I deserved. For the first time in a long time, I felt strong. Not because I had won any battle. Not because I had proved anything to anyone. I had finally chosen myself, and that was the most powerful decision I had ever made. And I will never hand that power away again.

* * *

YOUR TURN TO HEAL

1. What's one area of your life where you've been waiting for someone to understand, validate, or change?

_____

_____

_____

_____

_____
_____
_____
_____
_____
_____
_____
_____
_____
_____
_____
_____
_____
_____
_____

2. What would it look like to choose your peace over their approval?

_____
_____
_____
_____
_____
_____
_____
_____
_____
_____
_____
_____
_____
_____
_____
_____
_____
_____

RAW EMOTIONS

Letting go can feel like grief and freedom at the same time. When you've spent years carrying the weight of someone else's approval, finally releasing it can stir up sadness, anger, and relief. Use this space to name those emotions without shame. What part of your power are you ready to reclaim—fully, unapologetically, and without permission?

CHAPTER 11
GOD'S PROMISE AND THE PRICE OF FREEDOM

O n the night I collapsed under the weight of my divorce, God whispered to me: "This will be over in a year." At the time, I couldn't see how. The court battles were just beginning. My lawyer told me to expect years of back and forth. The expenses were piling up, and every step felt like I was walking deeper into financial quicksand.

But I held onto His words. I had nothing else. Faith became my oxygen. His promise—my anchor. As the legal battle intensified, I began to see the subtle ways God was moving. Unexpected blessings. Strength on days when I felt like I had none left. The right people showing up at the right time to help me through. This wasn't just about an ending. This was spiritual warfare. I wasn't just fighting a legal case—I was fighting for my sanity, my child's future, and my soul's survival. For the first time in a long time, I knew I wasn't fighting alone. The weight of my circumstances tried to break me, but I clung to the belief that God was guiding me.

There were moments of doubt, moments where I thought I would never see the other side of this. Every time I wanted to give up, something happened that made me feel as if He was still in control. It wasn't easy. There were days I felt completely abandoned. Nights where I cried myself to sleep. Mornings where I struggled to get out of bed. Somewhere deep inside, I knew that what God had promised me was real. Even when I couldn't see it, I trusted it. Even when I felt alone, I knew He was there. I didn't know what my life would look like after this, but I knew one thing for sure—God was not going to leave me in this place forever. Even in the courtroom, I knew I wasn't standing alone. This truth alone was enough to keep me moving forward.

And God was true to His promise. Within a year, the legal battle ended, but it had come with a price. I would lose money. I would lose people I thought were friends. I would lose family members who believed his lies. But I would gain my freedom, which was priceless.

One of the hardest things about leaving an emotionally toxic relationship is that people don't always see the scars. They don't understand why you can't just move on. They don't see what you see, feel, and endure—the sexual infidelities, the constant criticism, the absences in times of family need, the ongoing emotional warfare that left you drained. I was still recovering from years of gaslighting. Years of being told I alone was the problem; however, deep down, I knew I was the escape plan they never expected to execute.

The process of freeing myself was not as easy as just signing papers and walking away. I recall moments during the divorce when he said things like, "I wish you were dead," and "Our son would be better off with the insurance money." In my mind, I wondered, "How could someone who once claimed to love me say something like that?"

There were days when the financial stress felt unbearable. Nights where I questioned if I had made the right decision. Moments when I wondered if maybe I should have settled, just taken what he offered, just given in to make it all stop.

I couldn't.

I refused.

I knew that my freedom was worth more than money. I had sacrificed so much to hold the relationship together. I had given up parts of myself to keep the peace, to avoid the fights, to be the woman I thought he wanted me to be.

Not anymore.

The cost of staying was greater than the cost of leaving. So, I fought. I stood my ground. I refused to let him take any more from me. When the dust settled, when the papers were signed, when the legal battle was finally over, I stood there realizing that for the first time in years, I belonged to myself again. It wasn't just about winning in court, because trust me—I gave up a lot, including financial support for my child. It was about reclaiming my life. That victory was worth everything. No longer owned by fear. No longer silenced by guilt. No longer waiting for someone else's approval. I stood there realizing that for the first time in years, I belonged to myself again.

* * *

YOUR TURN TO HEAL

1. What "freedom" are you fighting for, even if it comes at a price?

_____
_____
_____
_____
_____
_____
_____
_____
_____
_____

2. What promise from God are you holding onto in the midst of uncertainty?

_____
_____
_____
_____
_____

_____
_____
_____
_____
_____

RAW EMOTIONS

Sometimes healing feels like loss before it feels like liberation. Take a
moment to reflect on what this chapter stirred up in you. Are you
grieving something you had to give up to gain your freedom? Are you
holding onto a promise that feels distant? Use this space to release
every raw, unfiltered emotion. This is your place to be fully honest
with what it has cost you to finally belong to yourself again.

_____
_____
_____
_____
_____
_____
_____
_____
_____
_____
_____
_____
_____
_____
_____
_____
_____
_____
_____
_____
_____
_____

RAW EMOTIONS

THE IMPORTANCE OF FORGIVENESS

Forgiveness was something I wrestled with for a long time.
I didn't want to forgive him.
I didn't want to release the anger, the resentment, the deep
*   sense of betrayal that had taken root inside me.*

I wanted justice.
I wanted accountability.
I wanted him to feel even a fraction of the pain he had
*   caused me.*
But I also wanted peace, which doesn't come from holding onto
*   bitterness.*

It wasn't about excusing what he did.
It wasn't about pretending it didn't hurt.

Forgiveness was for me.

It was about releasing the grip his actions had on my spirit.
It was about choosing my healing over my anger.

It was about freeing myself from the burden of carrying the past with me.

The moment I forgave him, I felt lighter.
It didn't mean I forgot.
It didn't mean I allowed him back into my life.
It meant that I was no longer bound to the pain he had inflicted.

Forgiveness was my final act of self-love.

CHAPTER 12
THE SILENCE THAT SPOKE
THE LOUDEST

For years, I craved validation. I just wanted someone to say, "I see you." Not the curated version. Not the photos. Me. But that moment never came. The highlight reel I posted on social media was just that—a reel. I longed for someone to look me in the eyes and say, "I see you. I believe you."

But that moment was slow to come.

He had time on his side. Time to shape the story. Time to plant seeds. I later learned through quiet conversations with friends that he had been telling stories for years. He had painted me as the angry one. The jealous one. The abuser. And the worst part? He did it slowly, so no one noticed the shift until it was too late.

I remember one day I called him and asked, "Can you start dinner and wash the dishes before I get home?" He said yes. But when I walked through the door, he was on the phone with a friend. The dishes were untouched. Dinner wasn't cooked. I was exhausted after working full-time and running a brand new private practice.

When I asked why, he snapped. Told me to leave him alone because he was on the phone. He acted as if I was the intruder in my own home—like my exhaustion was an inconvenience. Then, he called me rude. I lost it. I started yelling. I was exhausted, overwhelmed, and tired of broken promises.

As I reacted in frustration, I heard him say to the person on the phone, "She's always angry. All she does is yell." In that moment, I felt set up. The person on the other end hadn't heard the earlier promise he made to me. They didn't feel my exhaustion or understand the weight of my disappointment. They didn't know he had been home all day. All they heard was my anger. My reaction.

That scene repeated itself more times than I can count. He made promises. Promises to fix the car. To take out the garbage. To stop cheating. To work on his goals. And time after time, those promises were broken.

When the dust finally settled and he left for good, I stood in the silence. And it was louder than any argument we ever had. There were no calls. No check-ins. Just silence.

People I had laughed with, prayed with, built memories with. People who had known me for years slowly faded. Some became distant. Others seemed suspicious of me.

It felt like he had convinced them long before the relationship ended that I was the problem. He created a version of himself so convincing, even people who had witnessed his disrespect of me forgot what they had seen.

His mistress at the time began posting about our divorce and our son on social media. I was emotional. Vulnerable. Triggered. So, I called her—once. I asked her to remove the post and never speak our names again. A few days later, the police called me. They said she reported me for harassment. The officer admitted there was no evidence, but told me to stay away from her. I was stunned. One emotional phone call turned into police contact and a potential charge. In that moment, I surrendered. I had too much to lose. I changed the phone number I'd had for over twenty years. I realized how even the simplest defense in response to them could damage me or our son. I told my friends, "I made a mistake calling her." They agreed and helped me through one of the hardest moments of my life.

I found out later that he had given her my number. My address. He convinced her I called Child Protective Services on her, knowing it would push her to retaliate. He played us both. He set the fire and watched us both burn. He stayed quiet, kept his hands clean, and painted us both as unstable. As toxic.

He went on to start a healing organization. According to social media advertisements, he gave lectures to young men about emotional abuse and toxic marriage. He publicly announced himself online as a man who survived a toxic marriage and emotional abuse.

And people believed him.

I cried out to God. "Why? How is this happening? How could someone who mistreated me for so long convince the world he was the one who suffered?"

But, that is exactly what happened.

Worse than his betrayal was the betrayal of those who claimed to love me. I thought my heart was visible. I thought my loyalty, my work, my sacrifices would speak for themselves. What cut the deepest was silence from his family. From in-laws who had seen it all. The cheating. The disrespect. The disregard. They knew, and yet they said nothing.

I remember combing through his phone records. One number stood out. It appeared every day for three months. I confronted the woman on speakerphone while he stood there smiling, flipping turkey burgers. She told me the truth. She thought we had broken up. He told her we were done. He posted it on Facebook. She had met his family at their cookout. She had been courted. Dated. Treated like a woman in a brand new relationship. She called him her lover. I stood there, humiliated. Embarrassed. Hurt.

At one of his many parties, a woman walked up to him on the dance floor. She grabbed his neck, hugged him, and asked if he missed her. I stood three feet away recording the entire exchange. The people nearby looked at me and laughed. I will never forget the smirk on his face. How could I? I have it on video.

His family watched me work hard. They saw me hold it all together. They knew the arguments. The accusations. The times he left. The times I cried. Yet there were no phone calls. No prayers. No woman-to-woman compassion. Just silence.

That silence almost broke me. But God stepped in.

He stopped me from chasing their validation. He pulled me out of the fog. God is always working, even when it feels like everything is falling apart. He had to clear the space so He could rebuild something better.

He sent me women. Women who walked into my office as clients and ended up becoming mirrors. Women who didn't need to explain because I already knew. Women whose pain matched mine. And as I helped them, I began to heal myself.

I realized I didn't need permission to name what happened to me. I didn't need their approval to call it abuse. I didn't need anyone to confirm what I survived.

Because I knew.

And God knew.

And that was enough.

Even when they forgot. Even when they chose silence. God remembered. God saw me. The real me. The woman buried under manipulation, exhaustion, and fear. He knew that if I stayed, I would keep trying to prove I was lovable. So, He did what only He could do. He pulled me out. He exposed the wound. And He whispered, "You are going to heal. Without distraction. Without apology."

And that is exactly what I'm doing.

* * *

YOUR TURN TO HEAL

1. When have you felt betrayed by someone's silence?

_____

_____

_____

_____

_____

_____

_____

_____
_____
_____
_____
_____
_____
_____
_____
_____
_____
_____
_____

2. Has anyone ever distorted your truth?

_____
_____
_____
_____
_____
_____
_____
_____
_____
_____
_____
_____
_____
_____
_____
_____
_____
_____
_____

RAW EMOTIONS

Betrayal doesn't always come through words—it often comes through silence. Think about the moments when you felt unseen, unheard, or unprotected by those who should have spoken up. Let the emotions rise without judgment. What have you carried in the quiet? Use this space to pour out the anger, grief, confusion, or clarity that silence left behind.

_____

_____

_____

_____

_____

_____

_____

_____

_____

_____

_____

_____

_____

_____

_____

_____

_____

_____

_____

_____

_____

_____

_____

_____

_____

CHAPTER 13
REMEMBERING JOY

For a long time, I lived in survival mode. I forgot what joy felt like. I had spent so many years in survival mode—constantly trying to avoid arguments, walking on eggshells, managing my emotions to keep someone else comfortable. For so long, I had been navigating stress and uncertainty.

When I finally experienced peace, it took me time to adjust to this new way of living. At first, I didn't even trust it. I would wake up expecting tension, waiting for something to go wrong. My body still braced for chaos, even when none came. Out of habit, I would still prepare for the emotional roller coaster. I would catch myself hesitating before speaking, as if I still needed to measure every word.

Slowly, I started to breathe again. I found joy in the smallest things —drinking my coffee in silence without the weight of anxiety on my chest, laughing at a joke and realizing it was genuine, not forced to keep the peace, dancing in my kitchen without fear of being judged. Joy wasn't something I had to chase. It was something I had to allow myself to feel. Once I did, I realized that I had been starving for it all along.

I had to choose joy. I had to celebrate myself.

For years, I waited for someone else to celebrate with me. I waited for someone to acknowledge my hard work. I waited for someone to tell me, "I see you. I appreciate you. You matter." No one came. I realized I had to celebrate myself.

At first, it felt uncomfortable. Buying myself flowers. Taking myself out to dinner. Complimenting myself in the mirror. It all felt foreign, like I was doing something I wasn't allowed to do. But deep down, I knew I wasn't being selfish—I was being restored. Little by little, I started to enjoy it. I started treating myself with the kindness I had always given to others. I started speaking to myself with love instead of criticism. I started realizing that my worth was not dependent on someone else's validation.

Celebrating myself meant giving myself permission to feel proud. Acknowledging my growth. Honoring the woman I was becoming. It wasn't just about birthdays or special occasions. It was about making self-love a daily habit.

I no longer waited for someone else to recognize my value. I knew my own worth. That was the greatest celebration of all.

For a long time, I thought my pain had no purpose. I believed that everything I had endured—the manipulation, the shifting blame in conversations, the self-doubt—was just suffering without reason. I was wrong. God was using my pain to create something greater.

At first, I couldn't see it. I was too consumed by my own healing, by the effort it took to put myself back together. Slowly, I started noticing something. The more I shared my story, the more I realized I wasn't alone. The more I spoke about my experiences, the more I met other women who had lived through the same battles. Suddenly, I understood my healing wasn't just for me. It was for them too.

I started using my voice. I advocated for women who were still trapped in situations they didn't have the words to escape. I became a source of validation for those who had been gaslit into silence. I found purpose in my pain and strength in my story. I realized that everything I had been through had prepared me for this moment. I was no longer just a survivor. I was a healer. And healing others helped me heal myself.

* * *

YOUR TURN TO HEAL

1. What moments of joy have you dismissed, downplayed, or pushed away because they felt unfamiliar?

_____

_____

_____

_____

_____

_____

_____

_____

_____

_____

_____

_____

2. How can you start celebrating yourself without waiting for someone else to notice?

_____

_____

_____

_____

_____

_____

_____

_____

_____

_____

_____

_____

_____

RAW EMOTIONS

Sometimes joy feels uncomfortable after pain. It can feel risky to relax, to celebrate, and to smile without looking over your shoulder. In this space, let yourself name what joy feels like to you now. Write honestly —whether it's unfamiliar, overdue, or just beginning to bloom. What emotions rise when you remember yourself happy?

_____

_____

_____

_____

_____

_____

_____

_____

_____

_____

_____

_____

_____

_____

_____

_____

_____

_____

_____

_____

_____

_____

_____

_____

_____

_____

CHAPTER 14
CONCEALING THE HUMILIATION

ooking back, I realize I became a master at hiding pain. Wearing humiliation like a smile had become second nature. I masked it so well that most people had no clue what was really happening behind the scenes. I knew how to dress the part, smile on cue, and keep myself looking polished and composed because the outside had to look flawless. The outside had to say, "I'm okay," even when inside I was shattered.

Looking good became my armor. I kept my weight down, hit the gym, got my hair done, and dressed up no matter how broken I felt. My appearance became my survival tactic. It gave the illusion that my life was in order, that my marriage was strong, that I was fine. And sometimes, the illusion was all I had left.

And people believed it.

Some even liked me more because of it. Deep down, I always felt like they knew what he was saying about me behind my back. I felt like they knew what he was doing. I held my head high and smiled like everything was perfect. And I believe they played along.

Until the mask cracked.

I'll never forget walking through the mall with my baby and running into my brother-in-law and his wife. I greeted them warmly, smiling and making small talk. At the time, my partner was living in Texas, and I had been doing everything on my own.

Then she said it. I didn't see it coming. I never expected her to be the one to rip the curtain down.

"I'm tired of you acting like everything is perfect. Tired of you pretending you have the perfect marriage and the perfect husband. You don't. He cheated on you while he was in Texas. He had a whole other relationship."

Just like that. Right in the middle of the mall.

The humiliation I had spent years hiding spilled out with those words. And it wasn't the only time. He had so many relationships with other women over the years. So many moments. I'd see something suspicious on Facebook and ask questions, only to be met with silence or denial. On one occasion, I got access to his Facebook DM. I noticed a conversation he had started with a woman. When I began to communicate with her again, she asked, "What's the code?" Confused at her demands, I continued to speak to her without providing the code. She then stopped responding to me. I felt like none of these women respected me as his wife. Maybe because he didn't.

I never felt like he cared about being married. Over the course of our marriage, he lost five wedding bands. He always had a story. Said it fell off at work. Said rings didn't matter. Said he just lost it. And I would replace them every time, hoping maybe it would keep him grounded. Hoping it would tether us.

Then there were the parties he promoted. I often worked the door, collecting money—an important job that required someone he could trust. I handled the money. He handled the women.

But while I handled the front, I'd watch him from a distance, as he openly flirted with women. When I brought it up, he'd brush it off with, "It's part of the job," or tell me I was just being jealous. Still, I felt it deep in my gut—something about those interactions didn't sit right.

I remember one argument I had with a woman on Facebook after he publicly complimented her appearance. Their communication became disrespectful and flirtatious, and I asked him to shut it down. A month later, she showed up at his party. I was at the door, collecting money like always. He greeted her, walked over, and told me she didn't have to pay—right in front of me, like she was special and I was invisible.

I told him how much that moment hurt me—how humiliating it felt. But like always, he insisted I was overreacting, jumping to conclusions.

The public disrespect never stopped. And every time it happened, I swallowed it.

It usually happened at his events. I'd hold it in, wait until we got home to say something. I never wanted anyone to see me break. But, the cracks were there. I just worked hard to decorate them. I thought if I stayed composed in public, no one would see the truth of how broken I really was.

But, I was wrong. They saw it. They just pretended not to.

And when I confronted women about their actions, I never got an apology. No remorse. Just defensiveness—as if I was the problem. As if I was bitter, jealous, insecure.

I remember another party. A woman hugged him and kissed his neck right in front of me. I stood there frozen. When I brought it up, he didn't apologize. He said I was crazy. Like I imagined it. Like I was just being jealous again.

Working at his parties for years, I encountered two types of women. Some greeted me warmly and respectfully. Others looked past me and asked, "Where is he?" as if I didn't matter. As if I was in the way. I couldn't understand why they were so bold, so disrespectful.

I could only imagine what he said about me to them. Either way, I allowed it. I couldn't control it. My choice was simple: leave him or live with the humiliation.

The clothes and my appearance covered my torment, embarrassment, and shame at being treated like this. I wasn't strong because I looked good. I wasn't holding it together. I was just hiding how bad things really were.

Sometimes I wonder if I had allowed myself to look how I actually felt—exhausted, broken, worn down—maybe I would have left sooner. Maybe I would've faced the truth. Maybe I would've saved myself sooner.

But, I kept pretending. Kept smiling. Kept hiding. And in the process, I lost myself. Because I was too afraid to let the truth interrupt the performance. However, healing doesn't come through performance —it comes through permission. And I had to give myself permission to stop pretending.

* * *

YOUR TURN TO HEAL

1. Have you ever dressed up your pain to make it more palatable to others?

_____

_____

_____

_____

_____

_____

_____

_____

_____

_____

_____

_____

_____

_____

_____

_____

_____

_____

_____

_____

_____

_____

2. What would it look like to let yourself be seen—even if it's messy, imperfect, or raw?

_____

_____

_____

_____

_____

_____

_____

_____

_____

_____

_____

_____

_____

_____

_____

_____

_____

_____

_____

_____

_____

_____

_____

_____

_____

_____

_____

_____

_____

_____

_____

_____

RAW EMOTIONS

What have you carried beneath your appearance? Behind the polished image and perfect posture, what emotions have been tucked away, unseen? Use this space to name the weight you've hidden—anger, shame, exhaustion, grief—and let them breathe here, no longer masked or minimized.

CHAPTER 15

GIVING YOURSELF THE SAME EMPATHY YOU GAVE OTHERS

For most of my life, I poured every ounce of empathy into everyone else. I justified their actions, understood their pain, made excuses for their behavior, and carried the weight of their trauma on my back.

I told myself they couldn't help it, they were hurting, they were lost, they didn't mean to do the things they did.

Where was this same grace for me?

This book is not just for those who have suffered mental and emotional strain in romantic relationships. It is for anyone who has endured emotional manipulation—the kind that slowly erodes your identity while keeping you questioning your own reality—whether from a sibling, a parent, a relative, or a friend.

Emotionally harmful behavior is not confined to one type of relationship, and yet it is one of the most silent and destructive forms of pain.

We, as survivors, are often deeply empathetic. We rationalize the actions of those who hurt us because we understand that pain is cyclical. We convince ourselves that they didn't mean to harm us, that they were just repeating what was done to them.

Here's the truth: we are the ones who endured. If we are going to extend empathy to anyone, it should start with ourselves.

If you are going to make up excuses for someone's mistreatment, then use that same energy to defend your right to heal.

If you are going to justify someone else's actions, justify your own healing.

If you are going to spend your time understanding the complexity of their wounds, then take that same time to understand your own.

While you're busy excusing them, you are still sitting in pain. At some point, you have to make a choice. You have to choose yourself. You have to nurture your own wounds. You have to give yourself grace.

If you're going to endure the burden of gaslighting, manipulation, and abandonment, then let that burden at least include the ability to forgive yourself.

I won't sit here and pretend I was perfect. I made mistakes. I said things I regret. I reacted in ways that weren't always the wisest. I can now see how I allowed my ex-husband to undermine my worth, to magnify my mistakes, to make me a villain in both our lives. I internalized his judgment and let it shape how I saw myself.

Not anymore. I release myself. I forgive myself. I choose me.

I give myself permission to take care of myself the way I took care of others.

I give myself permission to be selfish, to be unapologetic, and to focus on my healing without guilt.

I give myself permission to love the little girl inside me, to nurture the grown woman I have become, to show myself the same compassion I gave so freely to those who never deserved it.

Here's the reality: when you are in a toxic relationship, you give and give and give. You give them understanding, patience, and support. You make excuses for them, bend over backward for them, explain away their cruelty, and convince yourself that they just need a little more love.

Where is the equality in that? If you look at a scale from 0 to 100, you probably gave them 90% of your empathy and left 10% for yourself.

Today, I give you permission to take back your 100%. Take care of you. You deserve this. You don't need permission from them. You don't need validation from them. You don't need closure from them. The only thing you need is the courage to prioritize yourself for the first time in a long time.

I remember the first time I truly prioritized myself after years of putting everyone else first. I looked in the mirror and made a decision. I was going to choose me.

At first, it felt selfish. I had been conditioned to believe that my worth was tied to how much I could give, how much I could endure, how much I could tolerate.

I wasn't tolerating anything anymore. Choosing myself meant setting boundaries even when it made others uncomfortable. Choosing myself meant prioritizing my happiness even when people didn't understand. Choosing myself meant finally, unapologetically, embracing the woman I was always meant to be.

For the first time, I didn't feel guilty. I felt free. Because choosing myself wasn't an act of selfishness.

It was an act of survival.

I would never again forget my own worth.

Because remembering my worth is how I begin again—every day.

* * *

YOUR TURN TO HEAL

1. Have you been more compassionate toward others than you have been to yourself? What would it look like to reverse that—even for one day?

_____

_____

_____

_____

_____

_____

2. What's one small way you can show up for yourself this week that you've shown up for others in the past?

_____

_____

_____

_____

_____

_____

RAW EMOTIONS

Think about all the mental and emotional energy you've spent understanding others. Now turn that understanding inward. What have you needed that you never gave yourself? Write it down without apology. Let this be the moment you offer compassion to the version of you who stayed, who tried, who survived.

_____

_____

_____

_____

_____

_____

_____

_____

_____

_____

_____

_____

_____

_____

_____

_____

_____

RAW EMOTIONS

THE WEIGHT OF RETHINKING

Some days come heavy.
Not because anything specific happened, but because you're
  sitting with yourself long enough to feel everything that
  used to be buried.

That's what today felt like.
I left the store, sat in my car, and the sadness came without
  warning.
It wasn't grief, not depression—just raw emotion.

It came in waves.
Deep thinking.
Rethinking.
Replaying moments I had to survive just to get here.

I have peace now.
I have healthy children.
A career I love.
Financial security.
I have everything I need.

And still, some days I cry more than once.
Some days I feel the weight of all the times I had to hold it in.
It doesn't stop me from functioning, but it sits heavy on my
      chest.
These moments don't ask for permission.
They just arrive.

Back then, I didn't have a safe space.
My feelings were dangerous.
They mirrored the abuser, so I kept them hidden.

When you're in something toxic, your focus is survival.
You learn to ignore your own pain to avoid conflict.
You swallow emotion to keep the peace.
You smile to avoid war.

But now, I have space. I have freedom.
And with that freedom comes everything I avoided.
Now I can feel it all.
And I do.

In stillness. In silence. In moments like this.
And as I sit with the memories and allow them to surface, I
      remind myself that this is part of healing.
This is what healing looks like.

Some days I move from sadness to peace within minutes.
Just a breath.
Just a reminder.
It's gonna be alright.

And honestly, alright is enough.
Alright means I'm healing.
Alright means I have another day to try again.
Alright means I'm still here.

PART THREE
THE BECOMING

This is where freedom lives—not because the past disappears, but because I've stopped letting it define me.

In this section, I embrace boundaries, joy, spiritual clarity, and the beauty of becoming whole. Every choice to love myself more deeply has moved me forward. So, if you're here, know that peace is possible.

You are becoming—and that is worth celebrating.

CHAPTER 16

THE POWER OF NO CONTACT, RECLAIMING MY PEACE

By the time the relationship ended, I wasn't just fighting to escape him—I was fighting to escape the version of myself that still craved his validation.

No contact forced me to sit with my own thoughts, my own worth, my own healing. It meant I had to rewire years of conditioning that made me feel like I needed him to feel whole. That was the hardest part—not hearing his voice, not reacting to his bait, not proving my side of the story.

But in the silence, I found my power.

Healing from emotional manipulation is not just about leaving—it's about making the unwavering decision to never go back. No contact isn't just avoidance; it's protection. It protects your peace, your mind, your spirit, and your future. It's about reclaiming your power in a way that words, arguments, or explanations never could.

For me, it was the hardest, yet most liberating decision I had ever made.

When you've been emotionally manipulated for so long, you become conditioned to seek validation from the very person who broke you. You want closure. Clarity. An apology—something that will make it all make sense. But the harsh truth is: that moment will never come.

I had to come to terms with this painful reality. No conversation would ever bring accountability. No explanation would undo the damage. No amount of words would restore what was lost. So, I made a choice.

I changed my phone number after two decades of using the same one. It was an act of self-care—a way to establish healthy boundaries and focus on healing.

I refused to let my healing be interrupted by moments of weakness or by the illusion that things could change.

Psychology professors and therapists have identified the behavior patterns of abusers: they cause you to question yourself and manipulate access to your energy, always keeping the door cracked. But when you go no contact, you take back everything they tried to steal from you.

There is power in silence.

I realized something profound—silence is not weakness. It's strength.

When I stopped explaining, I became untouchable.

When I stopped defending myself, I became free.

I didn't need to prove my truth to people who had already chosen to believe his stories. I didn't need to clear my name in a narrative that was designed to cast me as the villain.

I just needed to heal.

And that healing could only happen when I completely removed myself from the chaos.

If you're struggling with no contact, remember this:

- Every time you engage, you reopen the wound.
- Healing can't begin until the wound is closed for good.
- You cannot outsmart an emotional manipulator—they have spent years perfecting their skill.
- The only way to win is not to play.

- You do not need their validation to move forward. Their opinion of you does not define your reality.
- You deserve a life that is peaceful, joyful, and free. That life begins the moment you cut off their access to you.

No contact is not just about removing them. It's about choosing you —over and over again, every single day. And that choice is where your power lies.

* * *

YOUR TURN TO HEAL

1. Is there someone you've allowed access to your life who continues to disrupt your peace?

_____
_____
_____
_____
_____
_____
_____
_____
_____
_____

2. What boundary do you need to enforce to protect your healing— even if it's hard?

_____
_____
_____
_____
_____
_____

_____

_____

_____

_____

RAW EMOTIONS

Take a breath and sit with what this chapter stirred in you. Have you been holding space for someone who's already taken too much? Write about the emotions that surface when you think about closing the door for good—fear, grief, anger, relief. Let it all rise. This is your safe place to say what you haven't said out loud.

_____

_____

_____

_____

_____

_____

_____

_____

_____

_____

_____

_____

_____

_____

_____

_____

_____

_____

_____

_____

CHAPTER 17
EMBRACING THE UNKNOWN

When I was finally free, I realized that for the first time in my life, I wasn't planning everything. I wasn't waiting for the next argument, the next betrayal, the next moment of heartbreak. I was simply living. It was terrifying. I had spent so many years in survival mode that peace felt foreign to me.

What do you do when there's no crisis to manage?

What do you do when your life isn't centered around someone else's chaos?

What do you do when you're finally free?

At first, I felt lost. I felt like I was standing in the middle of an open road with no idea which direction to take. I realized something: I didn't need to have all the answers. I didn't need to know what was next. I just needed to trust that God had already paved the way.

Instead of running toward the next thing, I learned to be still. To embrace the unknown. To trust that whatever was coming would be better than what I left behind. In stillness, I found something I had never felt before—the beginning of my new life.

I won't sugarcoat this for you: embracing the unknown is hard. The process of rebuilding healthy relationships is painful. At first, you will feel like you have no one. You will feel empty, and it will be just you and God (or whatever higher power you believe in).

This part is necessary. This is where your foundation is rebuilt. This is where you learn to sit with yourself, to be okay with solitude, and to trust that the loneliness is temporary.

Here's what you have to understand: healing requires a clean slate. If you keep any emotionally manipulative people around, the pain of your trauma will always linger. Every time someone displays a familiar toxic behavior, it will trigger the same emotional wounds. It will keep you stuck in a cycle of reopening the same scars over and over again. You will never fully heal if you keep reopening the wound before it has a chance to close.

I encourage you: *don't be afraid to start over.*

* * *

YOUR TURN TO HEAL

1. What scares you most about starting over?

_____

_____

_____

_____

_____

_____

_____

_____

_____

_____

_____

_____

_____

_____

_____

_____

2. What if the unknown is actually where your peace is waiting?

_____
_____
_____
_____
_____
_____
_____
_____
_____
_____
_____
_____
_____
_____
_____
_____
_____

RAW EMOTIONS

What does the unknown bring up in you—freedom or fear? Maybe both? Let yourself write without needing to figure it all out. What parts of you are afraid of stillness? What emotions come up when you're not busy surviving, fixing, or performing? Honor the messiness of not knowing. That's where your healing expands.

_____
_____
_____
_____
_____
_____
_____

RAW EMOTIONS
THE BATTLE BETWEEN COMFORT AND TRUTH

*When you're healing from a relationship like that, rumination
  becomes part of your daily life.*
You think.
Then rethink.
Then think again.

You ask yourself, "Why? How? Was I really that low?"

*The answer doesn't always come quickly. Because in the
  moment, I didn't feel low.*
I didn't feel broken.
I didn't feel worthless.
But now, looking back, I can see how far gone I really was.

It's like living two completely different lives.

On one side, I was the accomplished woman.
The mother.
The leader.
The business owner.

The school psychologist with two master's degrees.
The woman who bought her own home, raised her kids, and
*   built a practice from the ground up.*
A woman of strength and grace, who kept going when every-
*   thing inside of her wanted to stop.*

And on the other side?
A woman who allowed deep disrespect.
Who accepted mistreatment.
Who stayed.

So, I asked myself, "How can both of these women exist in the
*   same body?"*
And the answer took me back to the beginning.

To the little girl who was taught that her feelings didn't matter.
The little girl who was taught to consider everyone else before
*   herself.*
The girl who grew up with a blueprint that told her love means
*   sacrifice—even when it hurts.*

That doctrine shaped who I became.
It taught me to prioritize others.
To give, give, give—without ever expecting anything back.
I became the support system for everyone around me.
The one who showed up.
The one who never needed anything.
The one who didn't ask for help.

And the truth is, I didn't even expect to be treated well.

My body ached for it.
My soul needed it.
But, I didn't expect it.

And your expectations? They shape your reality.

When you expect nothing, you'll accept anything — even when it hurts.

If I had had a father who showed me what love and protection looked like…
If I had seen what respect from a man felt like…
I would have never stayed nineteen years in that relationship.

That's why fathers are so important.
They shape a girl's self-worth.
They lay the foundation for what she believes she deserves.
They protect her and teach her how she should be treated.
Without that foundation, I grew up trying to figure it out as I went.

And even now, as a grown woman, I'm still battling it.
There's this constant tug-of-war between what feels comfortable — but is unhealthy — and what feels uncomfortable — but is right.
It's exhausting.

Comfort, to me, is familiar.
It's quiet compliance.
It's carrying everyone else's load.
It's silence instead of confrontation.
It's holding pain and smiling through it.
But, comfort has always hurt me.

And discomfort, as much as I hate it, is where I grow.
It's where truth lives.
It's where boundaries are built.
It's where I reclaim myself.

So now, I talk to myself every day.
I remind myself: "That's comfort. That's not right. This discomfort? That's growth. That's healing."

But, imagine that.
Imagine waking up every single day and choosing discomfort.
Choosing to sit in what feels unnatural because you know what
     feels natural will destroy you.

It's a battle I fight, daily.
And I think I'll be fighting it forever.

But, I also know this—my purpose is to help women like me
     heal.
To help little girls know their worth.
To help other women see they are not alone.

Because if I'm being honest?
I still struggle.
Every day.

But every day I choose to stay uncomfortable, I'm choosing to
     be free.

CHAPTER 18
BUILDING HEALTHY RELATIONSHIPS WITH BOUNDARIES

For so long, my toxic partner consumed my attention. His presence in my life was loud, overbearing, manipulative, and emotionally draining. He was the force that dictated my energy, my focus, my emotions. I became so centered on navigating, surviving, and appeasing him that I failed to see the other unhealthy relationships all around me.

These relationships had been there the entire time. They moved in silence, taking full advantage of my vulnerability while never stepping ahead of my ex. They hid behind his presence, allowing him to dominate while they played their own roles in my life—roles that, in hindsight, were just as damaging.

These people gaslit me, manipulated me, and drained me. But because they weren't as loud, I didn't notice. They picked at the pieces my ex had left behind. They took advantage in smaller, more subtle ways. But once I removed my toxic partner—once the distraction was gone—my eyes began to adjust to everything I had ignored. That's when I realized something life-changing: my ex was never my only problem.

Now, I want you to prepare yourself for this part of the journey. This is where things get lonely. This is where you start seeing people for who they really are—and it's uncomfortable. You're going to grieve. You're going to second-guess yourself. You're going to feel a deep sadness as you realize that many of the people you once trusted —the ones who stood by while you endured emotionally harmful behavior—were complicit in ways you didn't even recognize before.

Trust yourself in this process.

It's natural to want to hold onto every relationship, even the unhealthy ones, after your partner is gone. You might think, "I don't have anybody left."

But, let me tell you something: you do not need them.

You chose these people when you were still operating in survival mode.

When you were still adapting to dysfunction as normal.

When you were still broken and unaware of what healthy relationships should feel like.

Now that you are healing, you have permission to choose differently.

If you see characteristics of your ex in these people—even in small ways—trust yourself.

It's okay to let go.

It's okay to say, "I don't like how this feels."

It's okay to remove yourself from relationships that are not serving your healing.

You do not owe anyone an explanation.

But, here's the beautiful thing about this stage of healing: you get to redefine what relationships look like for you. The people who are meant to stay in your life will adapt to your boundaries.

They will respect your space, your voice, and your worth.

They will see you beyond what you once provided for them and love you for who you are—not what you give.

Pay attention to who is willing to change because they truly care for you.

Pay attention to who is willing to acknowledge their own behaviors and make adjustments because they value your place in their life.

Those, my friend, are the keepers.

Those are the ones you extend grace to.

Those are the ones you give the time to adjust.

Those are the ones you allow yourself to be vulnerable with.

Those are the ones who might even come back with a sincere apology—because they realize the role they played in your pain.

Now the rest?

Let them go.

Restart.

Regroup.

Revamp.

Rebuild relationships that are worthy of the healed version of you.

You deserve more than just surviving.

You deserve thriving.

* * *

YOUR TURN TO HEAL

1. Which relationships in your life need to be reevaluated now that you're healing?

_____

_____

_____

_____

_____

_____

2. What does a healthy relationship look and feel like to you—and are you willing to wait for it?

_____

_____

_____

_____

_____

_____

RAW EMOTIONS

Who are you without the people you once thought you couldn't live without? It's okay to grieve what's shifting. Let your pen be honest about the sadness, anger, or guilt that surfaces when you think about releasing old relationships. You're not weak for missing them—you're just human. But healing means choosing yourself, even when it feels lonely.

_____
_____
_____
_____
_____
_____
_____
_____
_____
_____
_____
_____
_____
_____
_____
_____
_____
_____
_____
_____
_____
_____
_____
_____

CHAPTER 19
TO THE WOMAN WHO FEELS STUCK

I f you are reading this and you feel lost, trapped, or unsure of how to move forward, I want you to pause for a moment and take a deep breath.

You are not alone.

I know what it feels like to carry the weight of doubt, to replay every decision, wondering if you're making a mistake.

I know the fear of stepping into the unknown—even when the known is breaking you.

I know what it's like to convince yourself that staying is easier than starting over.

I also know this: you are stronger than you think.

Healing is not about having all the answers today.

It's about trusting that you deserve more—even before you fully believe it.

It's about recognizing that prioritizing yourself is not selfish—it's survival.

There was a time when I believed love meant enduring pain.

That loyalty meant sacrificing myself.

That keeping the peace meant silencing my own needs.

I was wrong.

Walking away from what no longer serves you is not a weakness.
It is the bravest thing you will ever do.
You don't have to be fearless.
You don't have to have it all figured out.

You just have to take one step.

One step toward setting a boundary.
One step toward prioritizing yourself.
One step toward choosing a life that isn't built on pain.

And when you do?
You'll realize what I've come to know deep in my soul:

It's gonna be alright.

* * *

YOUR TURN TO HEAL

1. What is one small step you can take today to move toward freedom
—even if you're scared?

_____
_____
_____
_____
_____
_____
_____
_____
_____
_____
_____
_____
_____

2. What belief are you holding onto that's keeping you stuck—and are you willing to release it?

_____

_____

_____

_____

_____

_____

_____

_____

_____

_____

_____

_____

_____

_____

RAW EMOTIONS

This is your space to be completely honest. Are you scared to leave? Angry that you stayed? Numb from the weight of it all? Let it out— every raw, tangled feeling. You don't need to have the next chapter figured out right now. Just start by telling the truth about how this one feels.

_____

_____

_____

_____

_____

_____

_____

_____

_____

CHAPTER 20
TEARS OF JOY AND THE POWER OF SURRENDER

Throughout my marriage, there were countless days when I felt utterly defeated. The weight of my reality pressed down on me, draining me of any remaining strength. I would turn on Bible sermons just to get through the hour, clinging to the hope that God would send me a word—something, anything—to remind me that He was still with me.

I relied on God to function, so much so that I knew this was more than just a battle with my past. It was spiritual warfare. Every time I thought I had overcome one struggle, my ex-husband would challenge me with another, and I would again find myself on the battlefield—resisting his emotional detachment, mockery, or suspicion.

I felt as if to be married was to be at war, fighting to reclaim my life, my dignity, and my peace. I had pled for mutual respect, loyalty, and acknowledgment—for the basic courtesies that should exist in a loving relationship.

I remember what it felt like to beg for these things and be responded to with contempt in return. In the midst of my ending, God revealed to me how much I truly needed Him. I could not fight this battle alone. I immersed myself in worship, in scripture, in prayers that became my daily sustenance. I had friends and confidants, but even they could not fully understand the depths of what I was experiencing. Only God knew, and He sent me messages through His word— guiding me, sustaining me, reminding me that I wasn't alone.

This was not just a personal struggle; it was a battle of the spirit. My attempts to fight back with logic, reason, or even legal maneu- vering proved ineffective. This war was not of the flesh, but of the soul. The only way forward was through full surrender to God. It was in surrendering that I found true strength. When I allowed myself to be vulnerable before God, when I let my walls down, I was finally able to cry again—not tears of pain or regret, but tears of joy. The type of joy that can only be felt when you are truly free.

I remember walking outside one day, feeling the tears stream down my face, and realizing they weren't coming from a place of sadness. People around me assumed I was grieving, but I was experiencing something entirely different. I was crying because, for the first time in years, I felt the overwhelming presence of joy.

Tears of joy are unlike any other emotion. They come from the depths of your soul, from a place of pure liberation. People often talk about "tears of joy," but few describe what it truly feels like to finally be free from a burden that you carried for so long that it became a part of you. That kind of release is indescribable.

I remember praying one night, saying, "God, if my life were to end today, I am so grateful that You allowed me to experience joy." Grateful that He freed me from bondage and allowed me to experience peace.

It is difficult to fully experience joy if you are still living in bondage —if you are halfway in and halfway out, or if you have convinced yourself that suffering is your destiny.

God's plan was never for me to stay in pain. I believe He allowed me to endure it so that I could understand the depths of suffering to truly appreciate what it means to be whole again. Not just surviving, not just functioning, but excelling.

This is not the mediocre happiness that comes from a temporary reprieve. This is a joy rooted in self-fulfillment, divine purpose, and knowing that you are exactly where you are meant to be. This is the joy that cannot be taken away.

YOUR TURN TO HEAL

1. What would it look like to fully surrender your healing process to God?

_____

_____

_____

_____

_____

_____

_____

_____

_____

_____

_____

_____

2. Have you experienced a moment of unexpected joy during your journey?

_____

_____

_____

_____

_____

_____

_____

_____

_____

_____

_____

_____

RAW EMOTIONS

Let your heart speak freely here. Have you ever cried tears you didn't expect—tears that surprised you with their peace? Use this space to name what you're feeling right now, whether it's gratitude, hesitation, or even disbelief. Joy and pain often hold hands in the healing process —write down what's rising to the surface for you.

_____

_____

_____

_____

_____

_____

_____

_____

_____

_____

_____

_____

_____

_____

_____

_____

_____

_____

_____

_____

_____

_____

_____

_____

_____

_____

CHAPTER 21
EMBRACING TRIUMPH, TRANSFORMATION, & FAITH

Reflecting upon my journey, I am profoundly grateful for the path that has unfolded—a testament to resilience, determination, and the unyielding pursuit of purpose. As a young mother of three, I navigated the challenges of parenthood while steadfastly pursuing my education, culminating in the attainment of three master's degrees. Establishing a private mental health counseling practice in Harlem, I dedicated myself to helping people heal and also served as a school psychologist for over twenty-four years within the public school system.

I embodied the perception of a life "made"—someone who "overcame" the stigma assigned to young mothers. Yet beneath these accomplishments was a painful personal narrative.

Through these experiences, I discovered the transformative power of healing, turning pain into purpose by supporting and uplifting other women facing similar struggles.

Integral to this transformation has been the unwavering presence of God. Acknowledging His presence provides strength and solace.

In my journey, faith was the anchor that kept me afloat during the most tumultuous times, offering grace, mercy, and an enduring spirit. Today, my work continues with a renewed spirit—infused with joy and unburdened by past afflictions. I have learned that pursuing one's purpose need not be accompanied by suffering; instead, it can be a liberating journey marked by authenticity and fulfillment.

To every woman who feels ensnared by her circumstances, know this: your story is not solely defined by the hardships you've endured, but by the strength you've summoned to overcome them. Embrace your journey, for within it lies the power to transform pain into purpose and to live freely in the light of your truth.

* * *

YOUR TURN TO HEAL

1. What has your healing journey taught you about your strength and your faith?

_____

_____

_____

_____

_____

_____

_____

_____

_____

_____

_____

_____

_____

_____

_____

_____

_____

_____

_____

_____

2. How would your life change if you fully believed you were already enough?

_____

_____

_____

_____

_____

_____

_____

_____

_____

_____

_____

_____

_____

_____

_____

_____

_____

_____

_____

_____

_____

_____

_____

_____

_____

_____

_____

_____

_____

_____

_____

_____

_____

_____

RAW EMOTIONS

Close your eyes and sit with this truth: *You are not what happened to you —you are who you've become because of it.* What emotions rise when you reflect on your triumphs? Let yourself feel the depth of what you've survived, the faith that held you, and the version of you that's still unfolding. Write without judgment, just honesty.

_____
_____
_____
_____
_____
_____
_____
_____
_____
_____
_____
_____
_____
_____
_____
_____
_____
_____
_____
_____
_____
_____
_____
_____
_____
_____
_____
_____
_____

RAW EMOTIONS

SITTING WITH THE PAIN

This part of the journey is the hardest.
It's not the survival.
It's not the leaving.
It's the sitting with it all.
Sitting with the pain I avoided for years. Feeling everything I
*   once pushed aside just to make it through the day.*
This is the part where healing becomes real.
And it is not easy.

I look around, and I know I'm blessed.
I have what I need.
I've built a life I can be proud of.
But that doesn't stop the emotions from showing up.
Some days I feel so deeply sad.
Disappointed.
Not because I'm ungrateful, but because I'm processing every-
*   thing I've been through with new eyes.*

These emotions come like waves.
Some soft.

Some crashing.
And they don't always make sense in the moment.
But I've learned not to fight them.
I've learned to let them come.
Because they pass.
And when they do, I always return to one truth—it's gonna be
alright.

This stage is sacred.
It's quiet.
It's deep.
And it feels never-ending at times.
But I've reached a point in my healing where the pain doesn't
paralyze me anymore.
I can feel it without falling apart.
I can hold it and still hold myself.

I don't just want to survive.
I want to live.
And if I can do anything with this life I've been given, I want
to teach.
I want to pour into girls and women so they don't have to stay
stuck for as long as I did.
I want to show them the strength in solitude.
The beauty in healing.
The power in saying, "This ends with me."

So, if you're crying today, I understand.
If you're tired today, I've been there.
If you're overwhelmed by your own thoughts, know that I've
sat with mine, too.

And we're still here. Still healing. Still moving. And that alone
is worth everything.

STEPPING INTO THE LIGHT

I f you've made it to this point, then you've walked with me through the darkest valleys—through the weight of mental and emotional strain, manipulation, and betrayal. You've seen the moments when I felt like I wouldn't survive, when I questioned my worth, my sanity, my strength. If there is one thing I need you to know as you turn this final page, it's this: you will survive too.

Healing is not a destination. It is not a place you suddenly arrive at and say, "I am finally healed now." Healing is an active, continuous journey. It's waking up every day and choosing yourself. It's recognizing your patterns, making different choices, and learning to trust yourself again. It's understanding that what happened to you does not define how you rise from it.

For so long, I felt trapped in cycles, expectations—a story that wasn't mine to carry. But the truth is, the moment I decided to reclaim my voice, my power, my self-worth, I was no longer trapped. Neither are you.

If you're still in the process of leaving, if you're in the thick of healing, if you're just beginning to realize that you deserve more, I want you to hold onto this truth: you were never meant to live a life of survival. You were meant to prosper.

The scars may remain, but they do not have to define you. The memories may linger, but they do not have to break you. The people who hurt you may never acknowledge what they did, but that does not mean your pain was not real. More importantly, that does not mean you are not worthy of love—the right kind of love.

As you move forward, I hope you find joy in the small things. The way the sun rises after the darkest night. The way your laughter feels when it is unforced. The way peace settles into your bones when you realize that you are no longer at war with yourself.

This book was never about staying stuck in the pain. It was about showing you that healing is possible. That life on the other side of psychological distress is more beautiful than you could ever imagine. That even when you have been broken, even when you have lost yourself in someone else's storm, you can rebuild.

I am proof of that.

And so are you.

So, as you step into your next chapter, do so knowing that:

You are *worthy.*
You are *strong.*
You are *enough.*

And most of all, *it's gonna be alright.*

RESOURCES

If you are reading this and find yourself in crisis, in need of support, or simply searching for a place to begin your healing journey—you are not alone. Below are trusted resources that offer mental health support, emotional wellness services, and immediate help during a crisis.

IN CASE OF EMERGENCY

If you are experiencing suicidal thoughts, emotional distress, or feel unsafe in any way, please call 911 or go to the nearest emergency room.

You can also contact the National Suicide & Crisis Lifeline— call or text 988. They are available 24/7 for free and confidential support!

FIND A THERAPIST

Visit Psychology Today online. Explore a trusted directory of licensed therapists, counselors, and mental health professionals in your area.

THERAPEUTIC SUPPORT & COACHING

It's Never Too Late Mental Health Counseling, PLLC
Website: www.itsnevertoolatecounseling.com

- An inclusive, trauma-informed practice dedicated to helping individuals reclaim their peace and purpose.
- *Offering services for individuals, couples, and families.*

Shift Your Journey
Website: www.shiftyourjourney.com

- A wellness community focused on personal growth and healing.
- *Coaching, courses, and resources for women navigating life after trauma.*

The New Hope Mental Health Counseling Services
Website: www.thenewhopemhcs.com

- A compassionate space offering therapy for those impacted by trauma, abuse, and emotional distress.

Psychology Today

It's Never Too
Late Counseling

Shift Your Journey

The New Hope MHCS

ACKNOWLEDGMENTS

First and foremost, I give all glory and honor to God. Without His grace, I would not have had the strength to walk through the darkest valleys or the courage to share my truth. Every word in this book is a reflection of His mercy, His healing, and His unwavering love for me.

To my children, you are my heart, my motivation, and my greatest accomplishment. Thank you for loving me through the hardest parts of my life and for reminding me, every day, of what resilience looks like. You've seen more than you should have, and yet you love with grace and forgive with open hearts. I am in awe of each of you.

To the clients I've had the privilege of serving: you inspired me more than you know. Through your stories, I found strength. Through your healing, I found hope. Thank you for trusting me with your pain and allowing me to walk alongside you on your journey.

To my friends, loved ones, and therapist Dr. A, who saw me even when I couldn't see myself—thank you. Thank you for answering my calls, sitting with me in silence, praying with me, and reminding me who I was when I forgot. Your love held me together in ways you'll never fully understand.

To every woman who has cried in silence, who has doubted her worth, who has smiled while suffering—I wrote this for you. You are not alone. You are not invisible. You are worthy of peace, freedom, and joy.

To myself, thank you for not giving up. For choosing healing. For being brave enough to start again. For writing this story when it was easier to forget it. For telling the truth. For becoming the woman you were always meant to be.

ABOUT THE AUTHOR

Tiffany M. Civers is a licensed mental health counselor in New York and New Jersey, a certified school psychologist, and the CEO of It's Never Too Late Mental Health Counseling PLLC, a group practice based in Harlem. For the past 24 years, she has served the Harlem community as a school psychologist in the public school system. She holds a master's degree in school psychology, a master's in school administration, and a professional diploma in mental health counseling.

As both a therapist and survivor of Narcissistic Personality Disorder (NPD) abuse, Tiffany brings personal and clinical insight to her work, specializing in complex PTSD and emotional abuse. Her memoir, *It's Gonna Be Alright*, set to release in August 2025, chronicles her journey from surviving a 20-year emotionally traumatic marriage to finding freedom and healing after her divorce.

Through her organization, https://itsgonnabealright.org, Tiffany provides free six-week individual and group therapy for women who have recently left emotionally abusive relationships and need support navigating their next steps. Her mission is to bring awareness to the deep, layered impact of emotional abuse and to ensure that no survivor suffers in silence.

To learn more, visit:
https://itsnevertoolatecounseling.com
https://itsgonnabealright.org

www.ingramcontent.com/pod-product-compliance
Lightning Source LLC
Chambersburg PA
CBHW051204120626
46547CB00013B/1200